S. CHAPMAN

SEARCHING
for
MORE

Published in the United States by
Alpha Omega Publishing Company
P.O. Box 353, Jackson, MI 49204
Library of Congress Control Number: 2018960595

ISBN: 978-1-7320586-7-5

All Scripture quotations are derived from the Holy Bible.

Alpha Omega Publishing Company publishes books that promote the discussion and understanding of the Pentecostal movement throughout the world since the day of Pentecost. These books are made possible by the enthusiasm of our readers; the support of a committed group of donors, large and small; the collaboration of our many partners in the independent media and ecclesiastical organizations; booksellers, who often hand-sell Alpha Omega Publishing books; librarians; and above all by our authors.

Books may be purchased in quantity and/or special sales by contacting the publisher:

Alpha Omega Publishing
E: info@omegapublishing.org
www.omegapublishing.org

Printed in the United States of America

This book was a long time in the making. It is a collection of my wild thoughts refined by many, and without their time and belief in seeing this come to fruition, it would not have been. `

Thank you to Barb and Kathleen for the pre-edits, words of encouragement, and many laughs. Thank you to Antoi-nette for being a soundboard and my best friend. You and your husband have come up with more alternative endings to my writings than I have. I would like to give special recogni-tion to Brandon for reading and refining the first few pages in their earliest stage all while juggling law school and life.

Thank you: Barb, Kathleen, Antoinette and Brandon for actively participating in the progression of this piece of litera-ture in one way or another. For those who offered kind words, know they were appreciated.

This is my way of saying thank you for all that you've done.

It means the world that you believed in my vision for this book, and my dream of becoming a published author.

CONTENTS

PROLOGUE

I still recall what happened right before the gun fired. A man confessed to murder.

Odessa fainted; I swooped in to catch her. I turned my back for maybe three seconds and when I turned back around, I heard the gun go off. The end of the barrel was pointed in my direction, but it had not registered yet that I'd been shot. Lance's eyes were wide, and the panic on his face confirmed what I speculated. I felt the blood clinging to my shirt and touched the spot to make sure it was real. It was. Shock took over and I could not control my limbs...falling to my knees, then onto my side. Lance was kneeling beside me, and Odessa stood nearby.

The murderer was escaping. I didn't know if this was where I would die but I knew I'd had enough adventure and love in these past few months to satisfy my soul if it was. Just before blacking out, I heard Odessa talking to the emergency operator. "Officer, my friend was shot. Send help!" Those were the last words I heard before it all went away.

My mom always asked me if I thought I was indestructible whenever I did something reckless. I always wanted to tell her, *No, I know I am human and might be hurt or killed, I just do not care.* Well, today might have very well been my last day, and I cared.

I honestly would not have minded the great adventure and its conclusion a few months prior. Now all I craved was quiet moments, church, and time with the people I love, who happen to be the reason why I was shot. It transpired after meeting Lance, who shortly introduced me to Odessa, a runaway child. How did it happen? I'm still asking myself that same question. Time crept by in those final moments.

CHAPTER I

Arizona looks out her bedroom window, reflecting on her life. While lost in thought, her stomach churns with anticipation. This feeling in the pit of her stomach makes her uneasy all morning. Her initial thoughts circle around the romantic novel she finished the night before. Much later, when the feeling persists, she grows increasingly irritated and a little curious. Instead of passing it off as an upset stomach or ignoring it altogether—as if that were possible—she explores the possibilities. The feeling reminds her of the cliché "butterflies in your stomach", although she is not in love, or even in strong like with anyone. This feeling prompts Arizona to reminisce about the only person who can remind her of the butterflies she once had—Kurt Slone. Occasionally, she recalls Kurt. Not constantly, but when he arrives, his memory is unrelenting. Could he be the reason for tonight's funny feeling?

Arizona and Kurt met during their freshman year at college. Arizona hadn't noticed him at all until mid-semester when some friends who lived on the same floor as Kurt started mentioning him. Their friendship started as polite conversation when they saw each other in passing, which was sparingly. She visited her friends' floor frequently, either to play cards, watch movies, study or hang out. Whether by chance or by fate, they had all became friends. He played cards with the gang only a handful of times that entire school year. She and her friends would jokingly compare seeing Kurt to a Bigfoot sighting. He'd been big into his studies, and because of that no one saw much of him. And yet he managed to integrate himself into her social circle. At the end of freshman year, the various members in the gang exchanged numbers.

This led to Arizona answering an unknown number mid-summer. The rustic voice on the other end had exclaimed, "Hey, how's your summer going?" She'd been dumbfounded to hear Kurt's voice. He had seemed just as stunned to hear her brashly ask, "How did you get my number?"

The summer after her first year was the start of Arizona and Kurt's story, a painful story. One that is, to this day, hard for her to talk about. To help herself gain closure, on three separate occasions, she let her hand write what her heart felt for him. Twice she threw the papers away hoping to throw away the memories of him along with them. It worked, until she started to believe he was gone. That's when he crept back into her subconscious. Reminding her of his kindness, and the way conversation with him seemed to be effortless, even when he challenged her with difficult questions. She was reminded of how important she felt around him. When she thought back on their years of friendship and how significant he had become to her, she hated herself that much more. She hated how she let him creep into her heart and make a home there, only to vacate suddenly, leaving everything behind but his physical presence.

Two years of friendship, laughs, and a painful separation took its toll on her. Maybe this fluttering is her body's way of letting her know that she cannot push aside her feelings. She has to face them sometimes. With a defeated sigh, Arizona writes them out for the third time, hoping this was the last time. She lost herself once to the only person who made her heart beat fervently and her mind race with possibilities. She was not ready to feel that emotion again, not without him there to cultivate it.

Arizona does not want to remember Kurt and tries to protect herself emotionally. She never cries, rarely gets angry, and never allows herself to want something that anyone else has. She feels emotions are a waste of time. She wishes she could be absolved from them. Unfortunately, she is human, and she does have emotions. She spent the better part of her youth being an emotional wreck. She used to want to be someone else. She used to wish for things that could never happen. She cried for no reason and acted like a spoiled brat when she did not get her way. Arizona used to let her emotions drive her actions.

Since then, she learned that emotions should be shown less frequently, if at all. She did not have bad days; she was not allowed to. On good days, every day, she laughs a lot, often times at things only funny to herself. Despite the depressing, irrational desire to be devoid of emotions, she masks her true self and plays the role of a happy person; to appear content simplifies things. Most people do not get the opportunity to see how intelligent she is or how serious she can be when she speaks. She covers up the deeper parts of herself with jokes and silly comments. No one saw her angry side; that was reserved for the sixteen walls of her home.

She stomps around, bouncing from one room to the next, talking to no one about upsetting events that had transpired. Talking about things was a last resort, because it only made her angrier, which she hated. Having an excess of one emotion never solves anything, and she knows that. In her current state of adulthood, she keeps everyone at a lengthy distance: coworkers, bosses, and family members. At this stage, she does not even have friends, and for the most part, only leaves the house when necessary. No one makes a fuss over how Arizona leads her life. No one knows how Arizona really feels, or who she really is, and she is okay with that. Honestly, most days she prefers it. But on rare nights when she is unable to sleep, her emotions slip out.

She lays awake wishing someone would press to know her, the real Arizona. The part of her that is more than the façade she proclaims to be. After these spells pass, she feels silly for her weakness. She reminds herself afterwards that she hates personal questions and would not even begin to know how to open up, to answer anything about herself. She cannot divulge that information anyway, not without believing herself to be cripplingly foolish.

Trying to figure out Arizona Báton is like trying to solve a Rubik's Cube. How could others know her when she did not know herself? Digging deeper took a certain type of brain power and patience. So, her true inner self lays dormant.

Her long, soft, naturally curly, black hair wisps across the middle of her back as she rushes out of the parking garage elevator and into her office building. Her bronze-brown skin glows against her flesh-pink blouse. She chuckles quietly to herself, thinking about the bald stranger on the elevator with the spidery eyelashes. *He seemed nice.* He looks into her almond eyes and attempts to make small talk by commenting on the weather. He could not have known her distaste for small talk, especially about weather. No one knows. She often caught herself talking about it in passing and would instantly grow angry at herself for doing that.

Work is lax today. The office is in a buzz over the upcoming company holiday, which means a three-day weekend. The special holiday policy, unique to this company, was already in effect when Arizona started working here three years ago. She never questions the policies. She just enjoys the extra "holidays" off, including the last Fridays in January, June, and July.

Everyone in the office takes off two hours earlier than the typical quitting time. By the end of the shortened workday, she is not ready to go home just yet; nothing awaits her there but sixteen walls. Instead, she walks out the revolving glass doors on the main floor of the grand office building and struts across the street to Duluth Center.

The Center is a grassy park-like area with a flattering slope that accommodates a large, cement stage at the base of the slope. At the top of the slope are bright candy-apple red, wooden chairs and matching tables, spread about in no particular order. Trees shade half of the tables, some benches, and a portion of the walkway depending on the sunlight throughout the day. Duluth Center sits on its own lot surrounded by businesses. On certain days, Arizona would open the window at work that faces the park. Often, the office would liven up with music that came pouring out from the hearts of soulful, no name artists.

With work ending and people happily scurrying home, Arizona feels compelled to do the opposite. She walks until her nude four-inch heels lead her to Duluth Center. She picks out a bench on the far side, sits down, closes her eyes, and takes a deep breath. Fresh oxygen flows into her lungs, expanding and deflating her chest in one long, fluid motion. The sunlight, peeking through the green leaves of the tall trees, shines bright. A small finch hopping around to her left catches her attention, as it looks for food. Near a garbage can, it pecks at small bits of garbage. She watches it for a bit, hopping to and fro in search of food. She studies it for a while. The longer it searches, the more she wants to help. However, she knows she has no food in her purse.

The bird hops closer and looks at her. Their eyes meet, and she knows she has to help. It goes on scavenging while she digs in her purse pushing past lipstick, pens, and her brown leather wallet until she reaches the bottom. She pulls out a

8

single oat kernel with a speck of power-blue nail polish on it. Arizona tries to scrape it off delicately, but it was on there for good. She does not think the bird will mind. Just as she is about to hand it off, the finch flies away with something long and white in its beak.

Arizona waits for some time, kernel in hand, for the finch to come back. It never does. Just before leaving, she strategically drops it in the space between the cement sidewalk and the grass on the side of the walkway opposite to where she sat. If it decides to come back, it will know that she tried.

Leaving the Center in her white Durango, Arizona makes a left on Fourth Avenue, waits for the light to turn green, then makes another left onto Expressway 94 South. Having only driven five miles of her journey home, she remembers she needs groceries. She exits the Expressway onto Six Mile Road as she normally would. Instead of turning right to go home, she turns left towards the grocery store.

Chicken breast, tilapia, broccoli, peas, spinach, brown rice, granola bars, cherries, and apples. She is almost done shopping for the items on her mental grocery list. *Just have to get almonds,* she thought. As she turns into aisle seven, she notices a man and a woman in their early twenties. Her first instinct is to head down a different aisle. After considering it, she marches down the aisle, realizing it is foolish to retreat. First, what she needs is in this aisle. Second, it is perfectly reasonable for her to get what she needs. She grows more reluctant as she moves closer. She thinks to herself, *Of course what I need would be right next to the children fondling each other*. As she searches through the selection of nuts to find a sixteen-ounce bag of almonds, she overhears them talking.

"I'm so glad you were there at speed dating, all those months ago," the woman says. "You know, a part of me wishes I could go back and meet you for the first time all over again."

A husky voice replies, "As soon as I arrived, my eyes locked on you. I was so excited to get to your table; I knew if I had just two seconds of your time, I'd…"

He stops mid-sentence, smiling as Arizona walks past. A strong part of Arizona wants to say *eww*! The weakest part of her wants him to complete his romantic declaration. She grabs the bag she is looking for, and heads towards checkout. Arizona loads her groceries onto the conveyer belt. She looks behind her to see the same couple. She listens carefully, hoping to hear more of their conversation.

"You are just the sweetest thing ever. How did I get so lucky?" the woman gushes.

He whispers something in her ear that makes her ashen cheeks turn pink and a smile spreads across her face.

Out loud, as if answering her question more logically, or maybe advertising to others, he says, "Right place, right time; speed dating at El Dorado on the first Wednesday of every month."

"Your total is eighty-nine dollars and ten cents," the cashier alerts her.

She pays the lady, grabs her things and drives home thinking about what she will make for dinner and what chores need to be done.

Arizona wakes up the next morning feeling anxious. She eats her oatmeal and fruit with the same strange fluttering feeling in her stomach as the other day. *What is going to happen? Or better yet,* she wonders, *what is happening?* Throughout the years, Arizona has learned not to ignore her gut feeling. She makes a mental note of it and pushes it aside for the moment. She dresses casually, instead of putting on professional attire like she would on a typical Friday. She dresses for the start of her three-day weekend putting on a pair of dark-blue skinny jeans, a dandelion-yellow cotton sweater, and a silver locket necklace her grandmother had given her on her eighteenth birthday. The necklace reminds her of a time in her life when things had been simple. It symbolizes a time when she was not withdrawn from the world and when she did not conceal emotions.

Back then, her friends and her life had not been perfect, but... let's just say, ignorance really had been bliss. Having started her household chores last night, she continues them now hoping to finish soon. All that is left are two loads of laundry and cleaning the bathroom. If she can get that done and is not exhausted, she will run some errands.

Four hours later, she is already exhausted. After folding the two loads of laundry, scrubbing the toilet, sink, and bathtub, and sweeping and mopping the bathroom and kitchen floors, she is done cleaning, and dog tired from it. She takes a break before paying some bills online and considers going out to pay the rest of them at City Hall and update her license at the Secretary of State's office. Instead, she plops down on the couch. Soon after laying on the couch, which comfortably fit the length of her body, her left arm droops off the side. She falls asleep within just eleven minutes. REM sleep is soon to come.

Dreams are a strange concept. Dreamers seamlessly find themselves in the middle of a story. The dream ends up not making sense, but yet, if interesting enough, they obsess about it until it does. At least, this was the case for Arizona.

Her dream begins in a skiff on the Sea of Galilee. In the dream, she awakes to lightning electrifying the darkened skies. She hears the boom of ear-shattering thunder. The waves rock the small boat up and down, back and forth. She is frightened, experiencing all the elements working against her. In her present circumstance, she feels helpless. In the distance, a light draws her attention. It does not look like it came from a lighthouse, but that is all her mind comprehends it to be. As she focuses on the light, a peace[1] that surpasses her understanding begins to wash over her. Despite every obstacle that tells her, "You are not safe, this situation is dangerous," she feels comforted by the light. At first, she doesn't realize that the reassuring light was inching closer. She focuses her eyes trying to figure out if the waves were moving her closer. She is still unsure but is compelled to go towards the light. It does not matter what the light actually is; to her it means security. She flings her body over the side and splashes her arms in the water, using them to paddle onward, never taking her eyes off the light. She covers some distance but not enough. She fixes her gaze on the light, and instinctively stands up. The boat still rocks but she remains as steady as if she were standing on dry land. One leg at a time, she steps out onto the water without wondering if this was logical, or what would happen next. She just sees the light and knows things will work out.

She stands on the water and the waves where her feet are placed become still. The light is so close. Arizona thinks she can almost detect what it is. A faint voice whispers, "Thou shalt love the Lord thy God with all thy heart, and with all thy soul, and with all thy mind."[2] From the distance of half a

---

[1] Philippians 4:7
[2] St. Matthew 22:37

football field away, the lighthouse she is moving towards begins to look more like the silhouette of a man. In disbelief over what the light appears to resemble, she looks away. Lightning distracts her and in the blink of an eye, the water beneath her gives way and engulfs her.

She awakes, hurling herself up to a sitting position on the couch, having narrowly escaped a watery grave. After a long minute of disheveled dream recaps, she composes herself and walks to the kitchen for a drink of water. Through the window above the sink, she sees hues of sherbet orange. This signifies that no matter what the clock says, it is too late to make it to the Secretary of State's office today. Still she checks the time.

She walks to her front door and stands watching the vibrant sky. She takes note of the bold colors in the sunset. The orange sky has pops of purple. This transformation of nature puts Arizona at ease. No longer does it seem scary. In this moment, she soaks up its beauty. Arizona observes everything about the scene above and marvels. The curves of the fluffy clouds that move at their own pace, yielding for nothing, not even another cloud. The occasional flock of birds or plane that fly by. After watching the sun set, the view from her front door changes from a picturesque scene to the darkening sky from her dream. Arizona shuts the door, hoping to shut out those thoughts. She decides now would be as good a time as any to pay her bills.

Halfway through her online activity, she sees an advertisement in the corner of a webpage. If it would have been any other advertisement she would have ignored it, but because it is an advertisement for the El Dorado restaurant she cannot help giving in to her curiosity. Maybe she knows somehow or maybe she is strongly hoping that this will change the course of her life in some way. She apprehensively clicks on the advertisement which takes her to their website. There she quickly finds information about speed dating. Arizona's churning vanishes, and the apprehensive feeling subsides. After signing up, there are no sudden changes like she'd hoped there might be.

This was one of her classic impulse actions that did not, as predicted, produce enough adrenaline to make this moment matter. She finishes her night online, and though she is not yet tired, she dresses for bed. Indeed, she feels quite refreshed. Perhaps the nap did its job a little too well, despite the ominous dream.

As all the chores were completed, she decides to delve into a good book. She is careful about the types of books she exposes herself to. The emotional tornado the last book took her on was a strong enough lesson to make her cautious. Becoming personally invested in an exciting book could wreak havoc on her emotions. Knowing that about herself, she chooses wisely. She retrieves her Kindle and makes herself cozy on the couch. Her pajamas are hidden behind a snuggly soft blanket. She sits cross-legged on her couch. Exploring her library, she searches for a book to enjoy. *Nothing scary*, she thinks to herself. After all, the nightmare she experienced earlier is more than enough to satisfy her horror itch.

With that in mind, she disregards all thrillers, murder mysteries and anything close to those genres. *Nothing having to do with nature,* she thinks, shuddering slightly. She did not need an unwarranted reminder of natural elements such as thunderstorms, or water. *What does that leave me with? An epic love story, a classic novel, or perhaps a mixture of the two. Romeo and Juliet? No plays*, she tells herself. She searches for just the right story plot. Arizona finds something promising called *An Endless Moment*. When she reads the description, specific words stand out to her: love, faith, and family. She selects the book and settles in to read until her heart is content.

At the end of page 240, she looks up to see a dull light shining through the kitchen window. There is a blessing in being able to greet the dawn in this way, stumbling upon the morning's undisturbed grace while it slowly changes into the blazing light of day. The sun creeps up as the natural alarm clock it is known to be. Looking outside, Arizona surveys the beginning of a new day. Bird chirps come from all directions. A blue jay and a red robin sit perched on a nearby tree branch. As she observes the sun peeking above the horizon, the blaze of orange amazes her for the second time in less than twenty-four hours. She regards its beauty and then climbs up the stairs to her bed, leaving her Kindle and blanket on the couch. She lies in bed for a few minutes before passing out.

Arizona awakes to the sun peeking through her blinds, which she always leaves cracked open. She moves her head over slightly, so the sun is no longer in her eyes and lounges in bed enjoying the warmth and comfort. She thinks about *An Endless Moment*.

The story had begun with such a twist. *How Emily could agree to stay with a family she had never met before is beyond me. I do not know if I could vacation with a family I was not well acquainted with, let alone one I had never met before. The girl has more moxie than me. But they were kind enough. The family showed no ill-will towards her; they loved her, welcomed her, and made her feel a part of their family. What a beautifully fictitious family, never showing anger, full of compassion and laughter! I was completely enamored by their love for one another, especially towards Emily.*

She thinks about how she would handle Emily's various situations, putting aside reality and her self-inflicted character flaws. Eventually, Arizona concludes that fanaticizing about a world where things could ever work in her favor is not on the to-do list for today. She makes a mental note to pencil in daydreaming for her first day back to the office from her mini break.

She then remembers that spur of the moment commitment she'd made. "Crap!" she exclaims in a crackling morning voice that sounds like a frog's croak. She clears her throat and rises out of bed enthusiastically, pushing the white and black ink-blot duvet off of the top half of her body. The room-temperature air feels cold compared to the warmth under the covers. She does not factor that aspect into account when hastily exiting her bed. Expediently, she braces herself. Arizona reaches out wide in an upward motion shrugging her shoulders to their peak stretching-point for about seven seconds while her body adjusts itself. Arizona then heads to the bathroom to brush her teeth and get ready for the day. Two o'clock. If she hurries, she has time to make it to both City Hall and the Secretary of State.

Of course, the line at City Hall bends around the corner. Despite the length of the line, it moves swiftly. The building smells of mothballs and rotting wood. The aromatic atmosphere causes Arizona to recall the faint memory of her childhood visits to grandmother's house in Fort Ripley. *May she rest peacefully.* Her grandmother had been a selfless, kind woman. She always listened to Arizona's tall tales and had some of her own to share. They enjoyed years full of laughter and adventure.

Next on her list is the Secretary of State's office, which always takes longer than it should. She opens the doors to a large room with dark blue carpet, white walls and a long, large desk which separates the staff from the visitors. Five employees sit spaced equally apart, behind each three-foot-wide portion of the desk. Arizona grabs a ticket with the number thirteen on it. She looks at the number currently being served: forty-one. The long wait is a slight annoyance but nothing she has not encountered before. Arizona picks a seat and waits patiently. She watches the rotating video and safe-driving pictures that display statistics for a bit.

Her view switches between the now-serving number and the people all around her. Arizona notices a little girl, one row up and two seats to the left, who is kneeling on the floor playing with two toy dolls, a brown Barbie dressed in a fuchsia dress and Ken whose attire includes a light shirt and blue pants. The little girl is bouncing the toys up and down, parading the two around like they are having the adventure of a lifetime. Arizona tries to listen to the girl, but she cannot hear her over the mother, who is complaining about the long wait. Arizona looks at the number on the now-serving sign: fifty-one. Time in this place is a practical joke. Five minutes pass and it feels like an hour. The minutes drag and stretch themselves making sixty seconds seem like forever and a day. However, Arizona does not complain, as complaining solves nothing. Instead, she watches the girl play and thinks back to her childhood, her happiest time.

She recalls the Christmas she received her first dolly. It was a baby girl that came with a bottle. When the milk from the bottle was poured in the baby's mouth, it looked like the doll had gulped it all. The doll did not talk, but came with a diaper, a onesie, and a bonnet. She named the doll Veronica. She took that baby everywhere, but could not recall when she'd stopped playing with it, or if it was still around her childhood home. Arizona remembers wanting a child of her own. In those days, she used to pretend she had a family and her husband was a traveling salesman that was always away on business. She smiles at the thought of how she used to fantasize about the future. Suddenly, her smile contorts. Her expression grows solemn at the realization that the future she'd envisioned long ago was beaten into her present life. Enjoyment for Arizona takes effort, and often times she fakes it. She smiles, while mumbling inaudible words, or worse, thinking thoughts too callous for even the toughest heart to withstand. The life she wants requires love, which is the one thing that cannot come by force or under false pretenses. She takes an exaggerated breath while glancing again at the now-serving sign which shows that numbers eighty-one through ninety are now being served. Soon it would be her turn.

Finally, it is Arizona's turn. She walks toward the counter to renew her license. An older lady with blond and grey hair and a gap between her front teeth rambles on about her son's birthday which is the same date as Arizona's, the twentieth of January. She asks if Arizona gets stiffed on presents every year, receiving less Christmas presents because of her birthdate. Arizona explains to her that she never really notices because the gifts, whether plentiful or not, come second to spending time with family and the wonderful memories made. Arizona smiles wide, covering up her true feelings. *I bet this lady is eating this bull like it's birthday cake,* she thinks to herself. The desk clerk proceeds working while telling Arizona about what she did for her son on his birthday.

"Well, what we used to do was ask him to list his top four gifts that he really wanted, and we would give him two for Christmas and two for his birthday and sometimes when the money was really good we would give him some filler gifts as well."

"That is a clever idea," Arizona replies. "I bet he loved that. My parents bought me presents, but I mostly enjoyed the family time. My father was a traveling salesman and I knew I could always count on him to be there on my birthday. The mood in the house lifted whenever he came home. My mom and my sister and I were elated to see him."

"Oh, that's nice, you have a sister! My son is an only child and I always wished he could have had a sibling, but I couldn't have another child. My body just would not let me. It was a miracle I had him. What is your sister's name?"

Very quickly Arizona replies, "Veronica." She smiles, letting a chuckle escape as she continues. "Trust me, siblings are overrated. Veronica was always a baby; even to this day she still is."

"Must be a common trait for younger sisters, mine was the same way. She has also not gotten better with age," the clerk says.

Arizona finishes up her business and drives back to the house. Now that her errands are completed, she heads to the kitchen to prepare dinner. The growling coming from her stomach makes itself heard. She had not realized the extent of her hunger until now. She cannot recall what she's eaten all day or if she ate anything at all. Arizona grabs a protein bar to last her until dinner is ready. Her hunger has become more aggressive. *My stomach must be mad that all I can produce is granola and protein.* "Okay body, I get it, you're hungry," she says out loud. *Spaghetti is quick, easy, and cheesy.*

During dinner, once her stomach is sated, she remembers she has something bigger to worry about: speed dating, which she signed up for on a whim. She debates not going, *But then again,* she thinks, *what could it hurt to go?* She wrestles with the dilemma most of the night, weighing the pros and cons of going to the event. After talking it out to her walls, she decides she will give it a try. Now, all that is left to figure out is what to wear. Immediately, she pictures the red dress. She keeps a form-fitting, quarter-sleeve, deep-scoop-necked, knee-length, cherry-red dress hidden in the back of her closet just for such emergencies, like a date, or more realistically, a formal work event. She bought it right after college in her younger years when she was more hopeful. Now it gathers dust in the back of her closet.

She holds the hanger and regards the dress's beauty, hoping it still fits. To her surprise, after trying it on, it does. She admires the dress and notices how different it looks on her now compared to when she bought it. It looks better than she remembers. The curves of her twenty- five-year-old body accentuate the sophistication of the dress. She slides the dress off and returns it to the back of her closet. *Until Wednesday.* She dresses for bed and goes straight to her desk to write herself two reminders on a sticky note. The first reminder says:

El Dorado 574 Main Street

Wednesday 1st

8:00pm

On the very bottom, she adds:

(This will be a good experience!)

She writes the second reminder with both high hopes and high skepticism. With the reminders written down and in plain sight, and the outfit chosen, Arizona tries to anticipate what else needs to be done. *Shoes, jewelry, and hair.* She makes a mental note to figure out the right combination of jewelry later. The shoes are not a big deal. She plans to try on her top choices and decide the day of, while wearing the outfit. She heads to bed and drifts off to sleep mulling over which hairstyles would work best with her outfit.

She sleeps until the sun is in the center of the sky, basking in the comfort of her Egyptian cotton comforter, enjoying her bed to the fullest. Having previously completed all her chores and errands she just wants to relax before beginning the hustle and bustle that comes with her career. She tosses and turns, waking every so often to reposition, then begins dreaming again. By noon, the sun's rays poke through the blinds, positioned as they were, allowing a line to shine across her face, inviting her to join the sun party. She protests, pulling the covers over her head. Today is a day to do nothing. *Go away sun!* she commands. Then she smiles as she immerges from hibernation and realizes the beautiful thing about today. No fake smiling, no trying to entertain conversations with people, no mediocre interactions and most importantly, it is okay to stay in bed all day.

Realizing that today is a free day, meaning that she is free of societal norms, she perks up. Arizona is now ready to enjoy it. She bounces out of bed and marches downstairs, braless and with frizzy, wild hair. Arizona does not have a lot of friends and she likes it that way. No complications, no mistakes, and no being sympathetic to others' feelings. No having to pretend like she cares; that is the best result of her solitude. Arizona pours some Wheaties into a ceramic bowl then pours the milk and chows down.

After breakfast, she heads to the bathroom, brushes her teeth and then climbs back into bed. Laying there, she allows her body to enter into a relaxed state. Taking three deep breaths, she closes her eyes and clears her mind for meditation. After several hours, her thoughts and actions began to shift. She now commences a work-mode mindset by figuring out what tasks need to be completed, including whom she has to meet with this upcoming week and preparation for those meetings. She picks out her outfits for the week, eliminating potential wardrobe issues. She then meal preps her lunches, alternating between baked fish and pan-seared chicken. Of course veggies are included: peas and broccoli alternating with broccoli and carrots. Lunch would not be complete without jasmine rice. Once the meals are prepped, she rinses off the dishes and places them in the dishwasher. Cooking a week's worth of food leaves her drained. Here and there, she'd nibbled on the food, so she is no longer hungry.

Fatigued, Arizona turns on the flat screen television she bought as a housewarming gift for herself but rarely uses. She watches the news, and then switches to sports so that she will have something to talk about with her male counterparts in the office. Once she is all caught up on sports and news, she grabs her tablet. With a meticulous eye, she checks the overwhelming number of new emails, all of which are from various business contacts. Even on a day off, people still work. Checking emails takes up a huge chunk of time. It is now nine o'clock. All that is left to do is prepare for tomorrow by planning out meetings and assignments for the week. She selects her planner application and checks deadlines, adds a few more deadlines and includes preparation instructions for assignments that need to be worked on this week. Now that the leg work is complete, she heads upstairs to bed. Her mind races with work information. Tonight, she tumbles into a deep sleep and dreams of mergers, acquisitions, and winning the basketball game with a half-court free throw.

She awakes in a state of confusion, groggy from slumber. She staggers to the bathroom using the wall for guidance. The Monday fog hugs her and extends its hand of friendship. Seven o'clock creeps up on her as she showers, dresses, puts on her makeup, and brushes her curly hair into a loose bun on top of her head.

Arizona enjoys a bacon and spinach omelet which she'd prepared yesterday along with her lunch. She grabs her eggshell tote handbag, her work bag full of documents and jets out the front door. Her outfit choice for today consists of a knee-length, forest-green skirt with hip accent buttons on each side. The skirt came with a matching blazer, accented with the same style buttons, bringing cohesion and order to the suit. Underneath she wears a lightly textured, cream, sleeveless blouse. Her nylons frost her bronze legs and black, three-inch heels complete her outfit. There is no need for jewelry as the blouse comes up to the base of her neck and the blazer covers her wrists for the most part.

Arizona breathes in the crisp morning air, gaining an abundance of freshness that her home lacks. The pastel flowers that line her walkway and the grass, wet with dew, remind her of when her mother used to take her to school. During her adolescence, she believed the dew came from nymphs. *What foolish times those were*, she reflects. Swiftly, she sets her bags onto the passenger seat, positions herself in the driver's seat, and drives to work in silence.

Alone, she rides the elevator to her office's floor. She walks three steps to the left just before opening the doors to her department. She sighs heavily and places a smile on her face. *Today is the beginning of a successful and productive work week*, she tells herself. She crosses the threshold into her corporate world. Arizona wishes her job were more enjoyable but the work situation is convenient for her. It pays well, and the bosses and coworkers are pleasant. Yet, preforming the daily work-related tasks does not leave her fulfilled. Despite how unhappy she is, she does not complain; she is good at what she does for a living. She personally believes that work should not be fun. Work is for paying the bills, not for enjoyment. So, she lives day to day believing everyone just shows up at work because society tells them this is what you do. If you do not work, you do not eat.

Arizona's routine is the same every morning. She awakes feeling unrested and races against the clock trying to get ready. On her walk to the car, she considers the flowers whose colors appear bolder each day as the sun's awakening orange rays illuminate them. In a fluid motion, she positions her bags and gets in her car. The drive is silent, except for her thoughts which run through her schedule and deadlines for work. Before entering the office, she sighs and smiles, reminding herself that today is the beginning of a successful and productive work week and commences her job tasks. Some days are easier than others but the days all blur together regardless.

Naturally, time flies until the first Wednesday of the month arrives. Today, things begin the same with one exception. Arizona keeps El Dorado in the back of her mind. The red dress that was hanging in the back of her closet at the beginning of the week is now hanging up on her closet door, proudly on display. The black suede wedges she chose are resting directly under the dress. Her normally curly hair lies bone straight against her back. Throughout the day, she receives many compliments on her hair and when anyone asks why she straightened it, she answers, "I'm trying something different." She does not tell anyone of her plans for tonight. Arizona deems it an unprofessional topic and does not want people judging her. People tend to blow small things out of proportion; imagine what they would do with this information. No, Arizona does not desire to be the laughingstock of the office.

On the day Arizona wants work to feel like forever, it speeds by. Pulling into her driveway at 5:37 p.m., Arizona feels like she has only been away from home for a few hours, when in reality many hours have passed. She will never admit that her excitement got the best of her, turning the hours into minutes.

Speed dating starts at eight o'clock, leaving her with minimal time to get ready. She wonders if there will be food at the event. *Probably not since we are supposed to be mingling and not eating.* Arizona warms up some leftover chicken enchiladas. By 6:06, she is ready to begin the beautification process. Arizona wraps up her hair, and tucks it all under a shower cap before taking a shower. All the hours and effort she spent on her hair will not be in vain. Next, she grabs her soft-bristled toothbrush to begin brushing her teeth.

Now that she has showered, and her breath is minty fresh, she prepares her face for makeup. Arizona is no novice at makeup. She often fixes her face for work but does not get to experiment with more flirtatious styles. This is her night to take herself to a place of discomfort, but ultimately, growth. With the liquid eyeliner and a steady hand, she glides the brush across her top lid creating a cat eye. Then she moves south, painting her normally coral lips ruby red. She mentally pats herself on the back for donning her most daring makeup to date. She subtly applies pale-pink blush and a touch of highlighter to her cheeks, and her lashes extend so that when she looks up slightly they tickle her upper lid just below her eyebrow. She brushes her shiny black hair, which is waist length in its straightened form.

All that is left is the red dress. She walks to her closet, unzips the side of the dress and steps into it carefully. The dress looks stunning with her hair and makeup. Arizona stares in disbelief at her transformation. The uncomfortable feeling of being this *va-va-voom* sexy slowly subsides as she warms up to her appearance. Ten minutes pass then a couple more, and eventually she grows to love her sexy. She almost feels like a different person; almost. Lingering in her mind is the Cinderella idea, that when the clock strikes twelve, the magic goes away. But until then, she is stunning and ready for Prince Charming.

She wears her chunky gold bracelet, and her golden statement necklace. Now, the outfit truly comes together and all that is left are the shoes. The ones she'd planned on wearing no longer work. She scours the depths of her closet searching for her gold, four-inch stilettos with pointed toes that zip in the back and have gold ankle bands to secure the shoes to her foot.

"Ah ha!" she exclaims. "I knew you had to be in here somewhere."

Standing up and bracing herself against the closet wall, Arizona places her foot into one of the shoes. When trying to put the other one on, she wobbles trying to balance on a single stiletto. Holding steady on the slim heel, even using the wall for support, leaves her ankle shaky. She runs through a mental checklist: *Shoes, check; dress, double-check; hair and makeup, check; jewelry, check. My purse...* she debates the one she carries every day to work and while running errands. *It does not match.* She mentally searches her closet, although she knows she does not have a purse that matches. Sighing, Arizona leaves the house with no purse, just her keys, phone, ID and some cash.

Downtown is alive with bright lights, lively music of all varieties, and people enjoying themselves: restaurants, dancing, jazz joints, shopping, and comedy clubs. Arizona, who does not get out much, scans the pulse of the scene taking in as much as the drive allows. Quick stops make her yearn for more time to gawk. Her wish to stare longer is granted when she is halted by an ambulance fleeing through town, lights flashing, sirens blaring. Up ahead, police are redirecting traffic, but Arizona is in awe studying what the city has to offer. She shrugs off the authorities and passing EMTs, assuming this is typical downtown clamor. She appreciates that her impatience is rewarded with now being able to gape.

When she is just a few blocks away from El Dorado, seeing no available parking spots close by she is forced to park several blocks away. Hopping out of her SUV, she notes that she is parked across the street from a movie theater featuring *Exodus*. When speed dating is over, she will know exactly where to find her car.

She stands on the sidewalk, presses the button to activate the car alarm and feeds the meter. Key in hand, she glances at the theater marquee and reads the names of the other films playing. Carelessly, her fingers lose their grip on her key and it slips to the pavement in front of her. She looks down, then a man casually walking by sees this and immediately reacts. He reaches down and scoops up the key.

Handing it to her, he says, "Here you go."

She smiles. "Thank you."

"No problem," he replies, before walking off.

She hides the key in her bra and starts walking towards her destination which appears to be in the same direction that the helpful man is headed. She trails behind him and notices his sandy blond hair, cut low and very professional. As her gaze makes its way down from Mr. Helpful's hair to his outfit, he turns his head to see her walking in the same direction and staring at him. At first, he ignores her and turns his head back around. But as they reach the end of the block, he stops to let traffic go past and she catches up to him.

Hoping that this means something, she desperately speaks up. To Arizona, this feels like the beginning of a romantic comedy. "Hello again," she says. He briefly looks over, recognizing her, and replies, "Hello." He continues walking across the street, appearing uninterested in making more conversation. Arizona, on the other hand, is imagining her way across the street, planning what she would say next, and when she will say it. However, before she could come up with her next words, he turns right while she continues walking straight ahead. Feeling stupid for getting her hopes up over a stranger and their short-lived interactions, she tilts her head back to look up in regret, embarrassment clouding her mind.

Somewhere deep down inside, she believes that tonight will bring about the change she desperately craves. Realizing that she brought a hopeful attitude with her begins the deterioration of that hope. The heaviness of life she released earlier is gradually resurfacing into her awareness. Recognizing that she has high expectations, she expressionlessly strides on dragging doubt and hopelessness with her. By the time she arrives at El Dorado, her feet are throbbing, and she is sweaty from a combination of walking and nervousness.

El Dorado is a spacious Mexican restaurant. The yellow walls are covered in Latin American décor, featuring sombreros and Mexican flags. Mexican artwork is prominently displayed, and even the sound of chattering customers could not cover up Selena's voice. The song lyrics are in Spanish, but Arizona had seen the movie enough times to know her song "Dreaming of You" is playing. She had entered on the main floor, but in the middle of the restaurant three steps lead to the additional seating area. Both sections have the same light-maroon tile flooring.

The hostess, a young, petite woman with auburn hair that spirals down her back, is wearing a little, black, strapless dress with a peplum waist. She seats Arizona in the restaurant's upper section where other hopeful women sit. There are no men currently sitting down, instead they are standing off to the side waiting for the event to officially begin.

After a few minutes, a man in a white button-up shirt, black pants and no-slip grip shoes stands on a chair and claps his hands yelling, "Attention! Attention! May I have your attention? Speed dating at El Dorado is about to begin!"

The whole place erupts in a monsoon of cheers, hoots and hollers. The employee pauses to let them roar and then he continues yelling over the crowd, signifying he has more to say.

"But before we begin, I'll explain how we do things here. First, you will have five minutes to visit each table. Fellas, pick a table to start at, and then rotate to the next table on your right. Second, there are two pens and two pads of paper at each table. If numbers get exchanged, well," he said, smirking, "then it was a successful night, wasn't it?" A rumble rips through the group of men like the wave at a sporting event. A series of "Yeahs" and high-fives break out. Some women smile coyly, some laugh.

Arizona feels a shiver go down her spine as the man speaks. She knows it is a matter of minutes before some man will be breathing in her face, expecting to get lucky. She is so nervous that her thoughts run a mile a minute. Her imagination wrestles with itself. *What if he's boring, and we spend the whole five minutes staring at each other? Well, at least it is only five minutes then I meet someone new. Is it too late to slip out? Would I be able to get my money back? Oh crap, what did I get myself into? What if they're gorgeous and I forget how to converse? What if they're ugly? What if they smell, or have missing teeth?* She looks around to reassure herself that none of the men fit her fears. Quickly glancing around the room, she scans the potential dates and locates the exit just in case. She finds some of the men more attractive than others, but overall, not a bad group of men. She is a little more at ease, but her hands shake with apprehension.

The man on the chair finishes up. "And last, but not least, drinks are half price so drink up, chat away, and enjoy speed dating here at El Dorado."

Another man standing next to him, who is shorter than him even when he steps off the chair, rings a bell and the mingling begins. Men flood the floor in search of a table. Arizona sighs with relief at the first man to sit at her table. She's relieved that someone sat down at all, and that he is not bad looking. He even seems happy to meet her. A different part of her feels like she should not get her hopes up and realizes this event, and this guy, will probably never go beyond this festive table.

She projects a smile and plays the role of someone that is not damaged or uncomfortable. She acts as though she is engaged in what he is saying, laughs at all his jokes, but is glad they only have a short amount of time together. That means they cannot delve into any deep conversation. The first man introduces himself as Dill Gilbert. He seems a little older, somewhere in his late thirties. Dill makes a joke in reference to *What's Eating Gilbert Grape* and his name. The joke makes Arizona want to vomit. Seeing her expression of disdain, he compliments her dress. Arizona corrects her face, putting things back on track. Dill is not a fragile looking man, but his clothes disguise his slender frame. With the remaining time, they talk about the game on ESPN last night. The conversation reminds her of attending a company function. They both talk about individual players' playing style, specific players' averages, and recent trades. Time seems to glide by and with a loud, distracting warning, time is up. He moves to the right and the next man sits down.

They greet each other and exchange names. She tries to talk sports with her new date, Harold, since it worked so well the last time. Arizona figures if it is not broken, then do not fix it. But it is broken, as Harold could not expound on any sports topic she brings up. He apologizes for his lack of "common guy knowledge" and explains how he is an artist at heart. In his spare time, he often visits art museums and has painted a few pieces himself. None that he thinks are too awe inspiring, just portraits used as decor for his house. She sits and appears to listen to everything this man says, nodding her head and acting as if she's learning something. In reality, she hears his words and lets them escape from her mind. She does not need any free-thinking romanticized mumbo jumbo opening up her imagination to the possibility that she could be as free as he is.

She steals quick, hidden glances around the room. Looking at the others mingling and talking happily, she feels out of place. She attended this event with the hopes that something better would happen with her life. Maybe that means friendship or something more, but she knows she needs something to pull her out of the great abyss that life has drug her into. Instead of this being a reprieve from loneliness, she now feels more alone than ever. The abyss grows wider as depression sweeps upon her in a single moment.

By this time, the third person is seated in front of her. Arizona half-heartedly listens to his life story not even bothering to pretend she cares. She does not bother to remember his name or half of what he is talking about. Once the bell rings, she cannot even stand to stay in this place, and the fourth person sits down. Before he can utter a single syllable, she apologizes and leaves without any explanation. Arizona pushes on the restaurant's glass door to exit, but it seems heavier than it had when she entered. Just like this door, she feels heaviness upon her spirit, tugging and pulling her under.

The nighttime wind swirls lightly, sending her hair in every direction. Once it stops, her hair settles a little here, some there and she leaves it as it is. Her vision stays focused on the ground in front of her. Arizona walks towards her car. Her dress feels too tight, her skin feels too tight, and she feels as though she will burst out of it. This is not a new feeling, but still, it is not a pleasant one. People walk by, chatting. Arizona hears nothing but the gurgling noise of voices as she drowns in deep waters. She wants to scream for someone to help. At this very second, with lights blazing everywhere—street lights, store signs—it is all too much. She wants peace. In this moment, her desire to disappear intensifies tenfold. As Arizona reaches her car, instead of getting in and driving away, she crosses the street. She walks towards the movie theater, half hoping a car would grant her wish and it would all be over, especially the alternating dull and intense sensations she feels daily.

There is a small alley a few buildings down from the theater. She wishes to sulk in a place that offers her darkness to brood until this feeling passes. She walks in the darkness, void of everything. Tears streak down her cheeks. Sobs of melancholy cleanse her face of makeup. Halfway into the alley she stops, looks up, and through blurred vision, watches the lights taking over the sky dulled by the surrounding blackness. The taste of salt water seeps past her lips. The air wisps around her. Her hair again blows in every direction. She simply stares upward and continues to purge herself of tears.

Once her crying shifts to silence and her thoughts quiet down, she turns around to exit the alley. After a few steps in her walk of solitude, she feels something odd caress her ankle; it is cold and hard, yet flexible. She halts and looks down through sore, expressionless eyes that are slightly puffy and messy with eye makeup. With less than enough light coming in from the entrance to the alley, she struggles to make out what the object is. She can just barely make out a pale and rather large object attached to whatever she brushed up against. Arizona sees it twitch, an almost imperceptible motion, and her curiosity is piqued. *What is this?* She can feel its smooth edges. It kind of resembles a body part. She crouches down to get closer. *Are those fingers?* She moves boxes, trash and debris which hide the entirety of the mysterious figure. It twitches again, slower this time. She franticly pushes aside garbage and filth until she finally uncovers the mystery. Her eyes widen in horror, and air escapes her lungs, as she stares into the glassy eyes of a man. He winces and with a strained breath and a hoarse voice, he huffs, "Help me." Hysterically, she tosses off the remaining garbage.

In an attempt to get help, she screams, "Help, help, can anyone hear me?"

She takes his legs and swings them out, then grasps under his armpit to sit him up against the wall. He spits out inaudible protests between deep breaths. Through his tattered white shirt stained with deep-red blood, Arizona can see many blemishes on the left side of his torso. Clumps of dirt color his ice-blue face and pebbles leave indentations as they fall away. She checks his pulse, and finds it weak.

Arizona speaks slowly, her voice unsteady.

"We have to get you to the hospital, okay?" She pauses to swallow. A lump lodges itself in the base of her throat. "I'm going to lift you up and take you to my car. Do you understand me?" His head, which rests against the brick wall, rolls slightly to the right. Arizona takes that as a yes.

She grabs his hands, saying, "On the count of three, I'm going to pull you to your feet. Can you walk?"

He mumbles something incomprehensible, so she proceeds to count and pull. "One, two, three." She lifts up to no avail. "What's going on?" she asks him.

Arizona leans in towards his dry cracked lips, as he whispers painfully, "Can't feel legs." Terrified, she jumps up. "I'll be right back okay, please don't die." He holds a solemn expression.

Searching up and down the street, she looks for help. She knows she cannot do this by herself. To her surprise, there is no one in sight. She runs to her car, drives in reverse down the street and backs into the alley alongside the dying man. She leaves the key in the ignition and the car running. She runs to the nearest place that is open, a night club called Haute Imagination. *Bouncers and security guards,* she strategizes as she runs in and approaches the first strong-looking person in sight. She explains the situation to Joe who gets another bouncer to cover the front area.

She leads him to the injured man. Joe picks him up and sets him in the back seat of Arizona's Durango. No questions, no problem. He promises to call the hospital to let them know she's on her way. She quickly thanks Joe for his assistance then rushes to the driver's seat, and races towards the hospital. She darts through traffic, wondering *Where were all these people when I needed help*? The injured man groans in the back seat and keeps mumbling something she cannot decipher.

She dares to peek back at him. Blood shines in the passing light from street lamps that illuminate it. She realizes he is excessively filthy and in worse condition than he'd appeared in the darkened alleyway. Mounds of garbage piled on a dying corpse will do that. Whoever hurt him has done a good job of it. Horrified at the sight of this man and mortified at the sound of him she focuses on the road. For the remainder of the drive, she keeps her eyes forward. Within twenty minutes, she pulls up to the emergency doors of Kensington Hospital.

Arizona rushes through the doors, her face stained with tears. Shock and adrenaline keeping her going and blood stains almost blending into her dress, she alerts the registration clerk in choppy sentences about the medical condition of the stranger in her car. Three nurses quickly rush to his aid, load him on a gurney and wheel him off. In this moment, Arizona wants answers. She wants to know if this man is going to survive or not. She wants to know who could have done this, and why. But what she wants to know most of all is this person's identity. She feels personally drawn to him, which is undeniable. He witnessed her episode and essentially brought her out of her funk and into the fire. Arizona is not going to get the answers she desires by standing around. But that is all she can think to do.

As she prepares to follow after him, the nurse comes up to her and asks, "Are you related to that man?"

Arizona's thoughts are racing. She stands, staring with a blank expression, as her mind struggles to produce an answer. The nurse, about to repeat the question, is interrupted by Arizona. Still gazing at the nurse, her eyes still glassy, she blurts out, "Yes."

"Okay, I understand you must be going through a lot. There is paperwork I need you to fill out, but first you have to move your car." Arizona feels a ping of anxiety over having to answer questions. Especially since they are questions she wants answers to herself.

Before closing the rear passenger door, she notices a large black wallet on the floor under the driver's seat. The nurse is waving her on, indicating that she needs to move. So, instead of investigating now like she wants to, she closes the door, hops in, and drives to the nearest parking spot at the far end of the lot. She wedges herself in between two monster-sized Chevy pickup trucks. Before heading back into the hospital, she stretches her arm around behind her seat, her hand searching for the wallet. Finally, after a few blind swats at nothing, she is able to grab the wallet. With the wallet in hand, she repositions herself back into the driver's seat.

Arizona examines it before pulling out his driver's license, which read: Lance Nottingham. *His name is Lance Mason Nottingham, that's one mystery solved. Age 30, according to his license.* DOB 5/30, Address 4815 Oceanside Dr., Weight 180 lb. Eyes Blue. Still gripping the ID tightly, she drops her hands in her lap, leans her head back, and commits his ID photo to memory. Arizona dreads going back into the hospital. She is not ready to face the questions she will be expected to answer. Well, at least she has his wallet to help. She rummages through it to see what else she can find out about Mr. Nottingham. He is CPL certified, an organ donor, and does not have any cash. It is a possibility the money was stolen, but it makes more sense for someone to steal the whole wallet if theft was their intention. Prying through pockets, she finds credit cards. *Whoever did this was not after his money. This must have been some sort of personal vendetta. Perhaps he is a bad person who has wronged someone and is just getting the karma he dished out.* This makes the prospect of going back in there even less appealing.

Again, she leans her head back and thinks of his driver's license photo. A chill travels down her spine. Lance's smiling license picture turns into the pale, beaten face of the man she brought to this hospital. Arizona pops open her eyes, trying to lose the image, and looks out the windshield. The sky is lit from the entertainment district, but it is still dark enough for her to imagine the stars shining above her. She finds hope in the night sky, but it does not last long. Her peace is waning. She takes a heavy breath, burdened with what comes next. While lowering her gaze from the sky above, she catches a glimpse of her reflection in the rearview mirror. Her eyes jump from their sockets. With all the excitement, she'd forgotten her wild appearance.

She grabs the brush she keeps in her glove compartment along with some hair ties. Her phone falls out. She stares at it, thinking it would have come in handy earlier. She continues fixing her hair. A ponytail is formed within minutes. To tackle her face, she reaches for some napkins also in her glove box, and the water she keeps forgetting to take out of her car. Tonight, she is grateful for her memory lapse. Pouring the water onto the napkin, she uses it to wipe her face. Unfortunately, napkins disintegrate when exposed to liquid and friction. Napkin chunks fall from her hand, and bits stick to her face. Each piece she attempts to scrape away from her dress clings tighter. Ditching what is left of the napkin, she moves her flat palm across her thighs through the material of the dress with quick, hard strokes, to no avail. In fact, the already small pieces morph into smaller specks which spread out across her lap. Looking somewhat better, at least in her own mind, she sighs heavily and tells herself, "It is do or don't, now or never." She opens the door and slides out.

The adrenaline running through her veins begins to wear off, taking her out of flight or fight mode. The high of the night remains but is rapidly declining. She looks outward towards the unknown again. Maybe it is because of the monster-sized pickup trucks or the cloudy night, but she begins to feel microscopic. Realizing there is much at work within the universe, at this exact moment she doesn't perceive the large role she plays in her own story. The insignificance of her life feels as fleeting as the adrenaline. Still wearing her golden heels and the blood-stained dress covered in napkin bits that clings to her curves, she walks toward the hospital. Not with the desperation of trying to meet new people or suffocating loneliness. Instead, she walks into the hospital without a hope or an expectation. Placing one numb foot in front of the other, she presses onward into the unknown.

CHAPTER II

PART 1

H is eyes peep open, his body lies limp. The lightweight hospital blanket feels like it is crushing him. Every limb throbs with each *lub dub* of his heartbeat; from his pinky toe up to the tip of each hair, he pulsates with pain. Not one inch of him is unscathed. He is aware of the soreness first, however, the temperature soon sneaks up on him. The heat radiating around the room almost suffocates him. Antiseptic fills his nostrils and occupies his lungs, his chest painfully but gratefully rising and falling with each inflation and deflation. His heart pumps blood and pain to each nerve ending. He squints hard at first, then less and less until his eyes gradually open completely. The surrounding light is still too bright for Lance. He looks for the nearest reprieve and discovers a woman standing by the window gazing out. He observes her wild curly black hair while she focuses on something outside. He attempts to ask her to turn the lights down but his esophagus feels as if he has swallowed a cup full of sand. All he manages is a light cough, sounding faint to his own ears but just loud enough to catch her attention.

Arizona turns quickly. Bewildered by the sight of him awake, she stands frozen for a few seconds staring at his face, noting his eyes. This is the first time she's truly seen them. She grabs the Styrofoam cup filled with water sitting next to the hospital bed.

"I figured you would need this when you woke up." She places the straw in his mouth and continues to talk. "I had them bring you a fresh one every day."

40

Parched, he drinks the whole cup in one gulp. With a low, raspy voice, he patiently asks, "More please."

Arizona summons the nurse, telling her Lance is awake and that he needs more water. Looking down at him, she can see his breathing is strained and sweat is pouring down his face.

While peeling back the layers of blankets, she asks him, "Here, is this better?"

The nurse arrives and notices that his eyes are squinting. "I bet it's awfully bright in here for someone that hasn't seen the light of day in weeks." She turns off a few of the lights so that only one strip of light remains shining, leaving her enough to work with while protecting Lance's eyes. The nurse looks him over and just before leaving, she comments to Lance while glancing at Arizona. "You have healed so much in the time that you've been here, don't you agree?"

Arizona smiles at her and nods.

As she exits, the nurse adds, "I'll have someone bring more water."

Arizona's comforting smile reassures Lance that she is an ally. He does not want her smile to disappear, but seconds later it does. Fully opening his eyes, he has a chance to finally examine his surroundings and his friend.

Arizona resumes her reflective pose at the window, looking out at the night sky, too perplexed about what to say to actually say anything.

He looks around the room, trying to understand his situation. *Clearly, I was involved in an accident. It had to have been serious for me to end up here.* He has a better grasp on his surroundings excluding the owl by the window. He wonders who she is and why she is here with him.

Clearing her throat, Arizona's voice shatters the silence. "I can see the stars tonight. Clear as day."

He is already looking in her direction but does not respond. He half-heartedly attempts to look past her at the stars but cannot see them from the bed. He examines her while she faces the window. His gaze skims from her shoes to her curves, but mostly he looks at her hair. He likes how her wild curly hair sweeps across her back as she slightly shifts her weight from one leg to the other. He does not know how, why, or who she is, and nothing about this makes sense to him, but having her here gives him peace. Waking up from what appears to have been a traumatic accident forces Lance to disregard all logic, and in this moment, he assesses how he feels about the situation.

Deep in his subconscious, he believes she is important to his life and the reason he ended up here—alive. There is no evidence proving any of what he believes. All he has is his gut feeling and for now, that is enough for Lance. He simply stares at her peering out the window until someone comes in to bring him water. They set it down on the tray next to his bed and walk out. The nurse comes back to check his vitals and mark his chart. Once she's finished, she leaves them again.

"Don't mind her," Arizona directs as she reaches for the cup and places the straw in his mouth. This time she sits in the chair next to his bed and continues speaking.

"I snapped at her the night we arrived and ever since then, she has been either standoffish or snarky. Tonight she's both," Arizona explains. "She kept hounding me to fill out paperwork and I told her I was too emotionally distressed to fill out the forms. She persisted, so I told her rather abrasively, 'Lance has no allergies, and no medical history'. She backed off and after a few days, I realized you were not going to wake up and help me fill out the information. I told her I was finally ready to fill out the chart if she needed me too. She handed me the chart and I filled out what I could using the information in your wallet."

Lance coughed, water going down the wrong pipe. "What happened to me?" he chokes out.

She looks at him questioningly. "I was hoping you could tell me." She set the cup down and asks, "What's the last thing you remember?"

He looks at the ceiling lost in thought for a rather long moment. "I don't know, I can't remember."

Arizona suspects he will not know the answers to her next questions, but she has to ask anyway. "Do you know where you are?"

"The hospital?"

"Where at, which state?"

"I don't know."

"Do you know who you are?"

"Lance, I believe that's what I heard someone say."

Oh crap! "I was warned that you might have some amnesia once you woke up. I was really hoping you wouldn't." Arizona let out a defeated sigh just as the doctor enters.

"How do we feel," the doctor asks.

"Everything hurts, Doc."

The doctor spends a few minutes examining Lance. "That's to be expected as you've had three surgeries. There was some internal bleeding, as well as external bleeding on the left side of your torso, damage to the ligaments and your left tendon. And some fractures in your right hand. If she," he said, motioning to Arizona, who is sitting beside him, "had brought you in even a minute later, some of the damage could have been irreversible. But so far you seem to be healing nicely." Assessing his chart, the doctor adds, "We are going to need to test your motor functions and monitor your progress."

Arizona interrupts with, "Doctor, he doesn't remember anything. Is there something you can do to help? You know, medication or some type of therapy?"

He calls the nurse back into the room. "Give him Methadone, and 40 mg of Morphine for the pain." To Arizona, he answers, "As for his memory, we'll give it a few days. Perhaps you could bring in some of his mementos and photos, maybe tell him stories of some special memories you two share." Raising an eyebrow, he adds, "If that doesn't work, I can recommend some therapists who specialize in trauma-induced amnesia." He writes in the chart then leaves the room.

The nurse administers the pain medication through Lance's IV. "How does that feel?" she asks him.

"Better." The pain subsides and the nurse exits the room.

Looking at Arizona, Lance asks, "Hey, I'm roasting in here, could you please open the window or turn on the air; *something* to help me out?"

Arizona walks over and slides the glass pane to the left, letting in the brisk night air. "How is that?" Arizona asks.

"Much better, thank you."

An awkward silence fills the space along with the breeze. The unanswered questions and what they might mean weigh heavily on Arizona. Each of their thoughts remain their own. For quite a while, they look across at each other, neither of them wanting to speak first. Lance does not know what to say, and Arizona does not know where to start. Just as he is about to start speaking, he yawns and his eyes become heavy. Within a few minutes, he is out like a light.

The nurse monitoring from her station gives instructions through the intercom. "He's going to need to rest now. You can come back tomorrow if you would like."

Arizona complies and drives home with the intention of returning tomorrow just as she has every day since he was admitted.

Arizona is overjoyed that Lance has awoken and is recovering well. Unfortunately for her, he does not remember a single thing. She is desperately hoping to get some answers and on top of that, she will now need to find a way to explain to him that she does not know much more than him, other than how she found him left for dead in an alley.

She travels home from the hospital, as per her new usual, dresses for bed and attempts to journey to sleep, expecting the same dream that has occurred every night since she found Lance. Closing her eyes, she thinks about the latest development, elated that he is awake and unsure about how she can help his memory loss. She holds a lot of unwanted power. She could lie to him and make up some happy story. Arizona does not want to do that, but the truth is incomplete and leaves more questions than answers. She goes back and forth until she exhausts herself and finally drifts off to sleep.

The dream begins with an authoritative voice from above whispering, "Love," then pausing before finishing with, "thy neighbor as thyself."[3]

She stands alongside a dirt road asking, "Who is my neighbor?" A man appears walking down the road and she can

---

[3] St Luke 10:27-37

see his pockets overflowing with money and as he approaches a tree, Arizona sees thieves crouching behind it skulking about, ready to pounce. They rob the man and leave him wounded near the point of death. As he lays there dying, along comes a priest; certainly he will help. Yet, when the priest sees him, he walks to the other side of the road and carries on, never taking a second look back. Along comes a Levite, who glances at the injured man and continues on in the same manner as the priest. Then Arizona sees herself coming down the road and finding the man half dead, she is moved by compassion and meets him at his level. Bending down, she binds up his wounds and takes him to a place of rest. Before leaving him, she gives the innkeeper money and asks him to please take care of the man and that if more money is required, she will pay it when she returns.

The voice from above then poses a question, "Which of these three was a neighbor unto him that fell among thieves?"

Just like every other night she's had this dream, she wakes up hearing that question and the buzz of her alarm ringing in her ears. It's a work day, but good news! It's Friday. Everyone around the office perks up on Fridays, making the atmosphere much more pleasant. Contrary to her alternate life at the hospital, her usual morning routine is not interrupted. She spends a moment with nature, swoops into the car in one motion, drives in silence, and takes her customary deep breath before opening the doors at work.

She has not told anyone about her adventure at El Dorado, or about anything else from that night. Despite how much she wants to, Arizona still does not feel like that conversation is office appropriate. After work, she drives home, changes into something less mergers and acquisitions and more casual cute.

Making sure she brings her locket, she throws something on and focuses on more pressing matters. She has not given much thought to what she will say to Lance and is not going to stress herself out worrying about the unknown. The moment he asks her questions is when she will come up with answers.

Arizona drives to the hospital, anxious about seeing him. She kind of wants him to be awake but also wishes he will be sleeping. That will give her time to settle in and do more unnecessary deliberating. She parks as close to the hospital doors as possible, next to the one hundred handicapped parking spots. Ready or not, she walks into the hospital.

She peeks in before entering his room. Lance is on his back staring at the ceiling. He stops to look at her as soon as he hears her enter.

"Hey, I'm so glad to see you again," he says in greeting. "The only other people who visit me are the nurses."

Arizona moves toward the chair, smiling awkwardly and asks, "How are you feeling today?" She felt unsure about what else to ask someone in his condition.

"Still in pain, but what they've given me since last night really helps." He pauses before continuing. "I was wondering when you would be back. I asked the nurses if they knew. They said you visit almost every day." Proceeding cautiously, he commented, "I also asked them if they knew who you were; they said we're related, but not how. I was hoping now that you are here you could help fill in some gaps."

Oh boy, Arizona thinks, *we're starting this early, aren't we?* She picks up the cup of water from the tray in front of him and stalls, asking him, "Are you thirsty?"

"Actually yes, I tried to get it myself, but I can't really move too well." He answers with a huge smile. "My body is so stiff. I have been trying to do things on my own, but I have to ask

47

the nurses for a lot of help. The more I move, the easier movement becomes but it's a slow process. It just hurts more than it's worth sometimes. You know?"

Yeah, I know. She puts the straw in his mouth and watches him gulp down the water. "I'll have the nurse bring you some more."

"Thank you, I appreciate that...uh..."

"I'm Arizona."

Ready or not... She tries to figure out what to say next. *I guess that answers one of your questions...Try again... You want answers, right? No, that's stupid, of course he does! What if I say... no, that's not it. This whole situation is stupid. I am just going to smile until he says something.*

"That's a pretty name Arizona, I like it."

"Thanks, my grandma used to say I got my name because my skin was as dry as the Phoenix air."

He chuckles, and then there was more awkward silence.

She wrestles with her thoughts a bit more then blurts out, "How are you feeling today?" *Wait, didn't I already ask him that? Crap, is it too late to take it back?*

He smiles politely answering again, "I am still sore, but it is nothing like yesterday. That was true pain."

Arizona wants to correct him. If she were bold enough, she would tell him that true pain is not waking up sore. True pain is watching death take a ride in my back seat. It is waiting, each day, not knowing if your eyes are going to open. It is practicing what you would tell loved ones. Now that's true pain. Arizona is so engrossed in her fictitious speech she almost recites it in real life. *Oh, and another thing, pain is everything I just mentioned along with realizing at the end of it all how lucky you are Lance, to be absolved from the pain that I was going through. If only you understood my pain, true pain.* Lance interrupts her thoughts.

"We're not really related, are we?" Lance states more matter-of-fact then as a question.

Arizona can feel the sweat forming under her armpits. "What makes you say that?"

"You look too pretty to be related to me."

Arizona gives him a suspicious look that prompts Lance to answer seriously.

"I suppose it's an educated guess. You act like we are two strangers locked in a room, instead of siblings who spent our childhood together."

Arizona lets out a sigh and moves to the window. Lance watches her. This reminds him of last night, only today it is the sun that casts her shadow and not the moon's light. Lance breaks the silence.

"Is it that serious of a secret? I promise I won't tell anyone. Scout's honor."

When she does not respond he adds, "I believe you wouldn't have said it if there wasn't a reason to."

She still does not respond, and he questions further. "What are you looking at?"

Continuing to look out the window, Arizona finally responds, "Life will take you on some crazy adventures."

Lance thinks, *And how. I'm here in a hospital with amnesia, limited mobility, and some stranger who doesn't say much and yet makes me feel safe for some unknown reason.*

"I remember when I used to enjoy the little things, like a walk in the park, fresh flowers, and a gentle breeze passing by."

"You don't enjoy those things anymore?" Lance asks, puzzled.

She finally faces him and explains. "Yes, and no. I do but it's through windows and screens. I cannot remember the last time I stayed outside for very long and genuinely enjoyed it." After pausing to carefully consider her words, she continues. "I can't imagine what you must be going through. This must be incredibly hard. I am truly sorry."

"Don't be. It is difficult, but I'm blessed to be alive. Knowing the opposite was a very real possibility makes whatever I go through seem much more bearable." Lance's expression turns serious. "I just really wanna know what happened. Any information to help fill the void would be nice. Ever since I woke up it's like my memory is a puzzle and I have no pieces to complete it. Places, faces, it's just blank; what I know and who I know consist of these four walls, the hospital staff, and you."

After a long pause and a defeated sigh, Arizona tries again to explain. "Remem--" Just as she begins to speak, a nurse comes in to check his monitors and condition.

Arizona starts to ask the nurse, "When you get a chance…" But stopping mid-sentence, she revaluates her next words. "You know what, I'll go get it myself."

Directing her words at Lance she asks, "You must be hungry, right Lance?"

"Not especially," he replies.

The nurse chimes in, "That's the medication talking, you should eat something."

Arizona states, "It's settled. I'll get you some food."

He thinks for a second then changes his answer. "You're right, I should eat something. But you don't know what I want."

"Okay, what would you like?"

"I don't know, I will have to see what they have. Plus, I could use a change of scenery. Nurse, who do I talk to about a wheelchair?"

"They're down the hallway. She can grab the first one she sees."

Arizona steps out into the hallway, and hears the nurse say, "Turn left." She turns and walks to the end of the hall, but no chairs were in sight. So, she turns the corner and *voila!* There is a wheelchair parked facing a window, next to the door of another patient's room. Two nurses exit that room, closing the door behind them. On her way back to Lance's room with the wheelchair, Arizona ends up following the ladies and listening in on their conversation.

"That poor girl, I cannot believe what happened to her. Did you hear the story?"

"No, what happened?"

"The way I heard it, she ran out in front of a truck."

"Do you think it was a suicide attempt?"

"I'd like to think that it wasn't."

"How long do you think she is going to be in a coma?"

"It's tough to say. There's a lad somewhere on this floor who was admitted the same day as her, just a few hours later. He was in a coma but now he is awake."

They're talking about Lance.

"Oh, and I heard they were each found within a few blocks from each other."

51

"Some neighborhoods just aren't safe anymore. I steer clear of Downtown altogether."

"Same here. What did you bring for lunch?"

"I think I'm going to buy today."

Oh crap—lunch!

What with the new information she'd just heard, Arizona had forgotten all about why she left the room in the first place. After a few turns, she arrives back at Lance's room.

"Howdy stranger. I was beginning to think either the chairs were hiding from you or you went to the cafeteria without me," he joked.

"I was tempted, but honestly I don't even know where the cafeteria is."

"So, had you known where it was, would you have gone without me?"

Arizona changes the subject. "Where did the nurse go?"

"She went back to the nurse's station I believe."

"Great, I'll go get her. I need help getting you into this thing."

Once at the station, she gets the attention of the first available nurse and explains the situation.

"What room number again?"

"316."

"We'll send someone to help. Just wait patiently."

To Arizona's surprise, when she gets back to the room, Lance was already being assisted into the wheelchair by two nurses.

"Thanks guys," Lance tells them. Addressing Arizona, he says, "Are you ready?"

Pleasantly surprised, Arizona says, "Thank you," to both nurses.

One nurse says "Welcome" and the other one asks if she needs help wheeling him anywhere.

"Could you tell me where the cafeteria is?"

"Take the elevator to the second floor. You're going to make a right, then at the end of the hallway another right. There should be signs indicating where to go next." Both nurses, Arizona, and Lance all exit the room. Arizona and Lance make their way to the cafeteria.

She is apprehensive about having to explain things. *Will he demand answers now or wait until we get back?* Lance, however, appears to be happy just to get out of the room.

Pale walls and poor lighting await them in the cafeteria which is active with visitors. The place is not packed but it is busy. As she walks towards the food line, pushing Lance, she takes note of the food displayed. "Do you see anything that looks good?" She grabs a tray and they stand in line behind an older woman with fair hair and glasses and a younger man. The mother and son are talking loud enough for Arizona and Lance to overhear their conversation. Lance listens to them talk as Arizona scans the food choice.

"What would you like?" she asks again.

Too preoccupied with another conversation, Lance answers, "It all looks good, you decide." Arizona picks what she thinks he will find most appetizing.

Speaking to her son, the mother says, "Sarah is having such a rough pregnancy."

"The doctor said she has a bad case of preeclampsia," her son responds. "I didn't know what that was, so I Googled it. Google said it's high blood pressure during pregnancy."

"Yep, and in her case, it's getting worse." the mother continues. "That, plus her medical history. I mean, she told Abe she couldn't have kids when they first started dating. Now seven years into their marriage it is a miracle she is pregnant, but it is also taking its toll on everybody. Especially Sarah; she started hemorrhaging this morning. We'll have to keep that family in our prayers."

"Yeah," the son agrees, then adds, "I'm sure God has a plan. And his way is always right. In tough times, faith is the key."

Arizona finishes selecting the food and listens as the boy goes on. "Nothing that happens is coincidence. If God is allowing it to happen, He will bring them through it. It all works for His glory."

The mother and son walk away after paying for their food. Both Lance and Arizona cannot help but feel like they were meant to hear that.

Arizona is not against God. At this time in her life, she is not for him either. In her youth, her Grandma was the one who instilled religious practices, like going to church and reading the Bible. After her death, that was the end of that. Arizona grew up without religious education. She ponders the idea that maybe Christ is calling her back to him. *Nothing that happens is coincidence.* She silently pushes Lance back to the room.

Similar thoughts run through Lance's mind. *In tough times, faith is the key.*

The aromas coming from the tray make Lance's mouth water. The smell of the garlic on the mashed potatoes creeps up towards his nose. The golden-brown dinner roll glistens as butter slides down its surface. Even the meatloaf and corn look appetizing for hospital food. For desert, a chocolate-chip cookie. Arizona helps Lance get back in bed and wheels the chair outside of the room.

"This looks delicious! Is this all for me? Would you like some?"

Her answer is a solid, "No, I got it all with you in mind. I was hoping you would like it. It was kind of slim pickings, but it should do the trick."

"I think you are right."

In his hunger-induced state of mind, he rushes to grab the spork.

"Ouch," he exclaims as he is instantly reminded of his limitations. "I almost forgot that I'm in here for a reason."

Moving with caution, he tries again to reach for the utensil.

"Let me help you," Arizona asserts.

"I can do it. It's just I have to move carefully or else—pain." He chuckles lightly. "Movement is a slow progress. The doctors told me I suffered some nerve damage in both hands and my leg. I'll bet they probably told you that too."

"They didn't have to tell me. The night I found you…" Her words taper off and instead of finishing her thought, she adds, "I'm glad it's not worse." She hopes he catches on to what she's implying and prompts for more. When he does not, she changes the topic.

"Did they say anything else, possibly about recovery plans?"

"Yeah, they want to start rehabilitation tomorrow to test my mobility. It would be nice to be able to move freely." He glances over at Arizona then focuses on his food.

"Here, let me help."

She grabs the spork from out of his hand and finishes scooping up the bite of mashed potatoes. As she reaches down to scoop up another bite, he questions, "Where was I at?"

"Huh?"

"Where did you find me?"

She meets his gaze then drops her eyes when she answers. "The downtown entertainment district, in an alley down a bit from a theater."

"So, what were you doing the night you found me?"

Not knowing how to answer, she pauses, continuing to feed him, while thinking of what to say. Arizona did not want to lie but the truth is not pleasant.

"I was having a really bad time that night. I needed a moment, so I went into an alley to be alone. When I was ready to leave, I stumbled upon you."

He swallows his food, and then his voice fills the silence. "Is there anything else you can recall about that night?" He senses her hesitation and implores her to answer. "I'm drawing a blank, literally, about everything and you're my hope for answers."

His pleading eyes and tone squash any intentions of lying. She sighs, knowing what she has to do next. *Ready or not*. She speaks her next words slowly, each word guarded and deliberate.

"Every night that you were asleep in this bed, I was with you. I stood by the window and watched the night sky. When I wasn't checking on you, I thought long and hard about how and what to say. I questioned 'Why me?' and rationalized what kind of a person you were to end up in such a situation. I did a lot of thinking, but I never arrived at an answer to any of this. Every night I imagined what I would say to you when you woke up. I was dreading this moment because, honestly, I don't know much more than you do. That night started out so badly that I don't even want to tell you what I was going through before I found you. All I can say is that I found you in an alleyway in the entertainment district. You were in bad condition—pale as paper, and cold as ice. On my way out of the alley, I felt something touch me. You twitched and that's how I knew you were alive. I sat you up and you mumbled something. Actually, you mumbled a lot that night. Most of it I could not make out; I thought about that as well. Trying to discern what you had said that night, I couldn't make out any words, but I thought if I tried hard enough to remember maybe that would help. A man put you into my car. I drove you here. You mumbled the most on the ride here. I looked back at you for just a second, and could not look at you again that night." Tears are streaming down Arizona's face. "You were in my back seat dying, I felt so helpless. That night was pure instinct and adrenalin. I told the hospital staff we were related. And I've been here ever since. I had to know how this would end. I had to see this through. No matter the outcome, I had to know that you were okay."

She tries to be angry at herself for being weak and vulnerable, but realizes it is okay for her to be fragile around Lance because he is broken too.

Lance, comprehending they are in the same boat, lost at sea with no paddles and not even the North Star to guide them, places his hand on hers, comforting her enough to continue.

She speaks from a place of humility. "I don't know who you are or what happened to you that night prior to me finding you. All I know is that nothing happens without a purpose. You are alive, and it is not because of me. That night I looked up and recognized the world is bigger than I ever knew it to be before."

He takes his hand from Arizona's and pushes the tray out of his way. Slowly, he positions himself on the edge of his hospital bed, creating enough space for another person. He pats that spot indicating it is for her and she gives him a questioning look. He coaxes her, saying, "I did all that work, don't let it be in vain."

"Are you sure?" she asks. "I mean, we technically just met."

"Actually, I've known you my whole life; remember, we are family," he responds with a chuckle. "Plus, I never properly thanked you and since I can't get up to give you a hug, come sit and hug me."

She smiles, wiping the last of her tears from her blushing cheeks and red eyes. She kicks off her shoes and climbs onto the bed. He places his arm on her shoulder and she snuggles into him as much as the limited space would allow. She continues to be comforted by his presence. After a moment of rhythmic breathing entertaining their ears, Lance speaks.

"I don't remember who I was or anything really prior to waking up, but I can honestly say that being here today, alive, has a lot to do with you—period. You were right where you needed to be that night. You saved my life! I have breath in my lungs, and a heart that beats strong." He pauses, and Arizona can hear his heart's lub dub and feel the expansion of his chest as he breathes. She hears and feels his whispered "Thank you" in her hair.

She closes her eyes, now knowing where to begin. In a hushed voice, she reveals some of what he wants to know and what she has committed to memory.

"Lance Mason Nottingham, 30 years old, 180 pounds, blue eyes." She lets the information drift into the air and waits for him to absorb it.

After a moment of visualizing himself as Lance Mason Nottingham, a broad-shouldered, upstanding man of purpose, he speaks the name slowly. "Lance Mason Nottingham. I like it."

This is a moment of complete innocence. Arizona would have spent the next week full of self-loathing had he not embraced her fragile soul with his own and become her relief and she his connection.

PART 2

U nsure of what to expect, Lance waits and observes everything. After the nurse is done poking and prodding and leaves, he counts, waiting for Arizona to return. After she left yesterday, he made her promise to come back today. In the meantime, Lance discovers his knack for numbers. The ceiling tiles are his favorite objects to count, mostly because they are the only countable objects within his view. Earlier, he'd counted the exact number of tiles and now he wants to know the exact number of tiny dots on each individual tile. He starts by counting the tiny dots both horizontally and vertically in a single tile, then multiplies to calculate the total.

"So that's thirteen times sixteen which makes two hundred and eight. Multiply that by two hundred and twenty-four. Forty-six thousand, five hundred and ninety-two." Arizona arrives just in time to hear his calculations.

"Forty-six thousand, five hundred and ninety-two *what*?"

"Ceiling tiles; I like to count them."

"I should bring you a book to keep you occupied."

"What's wrong with counting ceiling tiles?"

"How many times can you count them before the math no longer becomes interesting?"

"Touché," he says. Then he asks, "How did you convince the staff that we are related?"

She giggles softly. "Wouldn't you like to know?"

"Come on, what'd you tell 'em?"

"Alright, here's what happened." She talks as if she is sharing some juicy gossip with a friend over tea. "So, I left *most* parts blank on the forms that the nurse gave me, and when they would ask about those sections, I would cry and ask questions about your condition, then storm off emotionally into a corner or to the window. After a few days, they came to their own conclusions and I ran with what they said. Admittedly, I've been a really difficult relative to deal with. I'm surprised they haven't kicked me out." She grins, and he grins back.

"There's still time," he jokes, and then asks, "They concluded that we're siblings?" Arizona decides not to mention their original suggestion, that she was his wife because of her attentiveness to his needs and perfect attendance at the hospital.

"Yeah, according to them we are brother and sister; we must look alike or something. Also, I added 'orphaned' to the description, mostly because I couldn't supply your medical history. Orphaned naturally made sense. It is the perfect alibi."

"Ah! Because we wouldn't have traceable medical history, I got ya."

"It's elementary, my dear brother."

"Oh, that's smart, little sis."

She turns back to his blue gaze and repeats, "Little? Sister?"

He looks up at the ceiling, resuming his counting. He stops to answer, "Yeah, you don't look a day over twenty-five. You know, I've been thinking and if you look closely, we do kind of resemble each other. Maybe we really could be siblings." They do not look at all look like siblings. His blue eyes, pointed nose, and pale skin are in stark contrast to her brown eyes, rounded button nose, and tan skin. This was another thing he'd discovered about himself—his lighthearted sense of humor.

She watches him looking up at the ceiling. She is surprised at how accepting he is of her tall tales, and how adaptable he is to the craziness he awoke to. Honestly, she feels a ping of joy when he calls her his little sister. She has never had a sibling. These days, the incessant fluttering in her stomach came and went. There is no denying that something big is soon to happen. For the time being, she embraces the person she is with him, yet knows reality is soon to break through this fantasy. *I guess it has not been as crazy for him as it is for me... What am I thinking? This has been a wild ride for both of us. This man almost dies in my back seat and lives only to realize he does not remember anything. I guess losing your memory is somewhat easy. Here I am with the horrifying picture of that night ingrained in my memory. And now here I am, the foolish one, coming back here, pretending I'm his sister, lying in his bed and almost falling asleep in his arms. Arizona girl, get yourself together, chump. Where does this go from here? We have no future. When all is said and done, I am going to be the stupid one, worse off than before for thinking anything good will happen to me from this. Today has to be the end. He is doing better; in fact, much better since the first night. I wanted to find out his state of being and now I know —alive and healthy. Just leave and let him figure out the memory loss on his own.*

She is just about to excuse herself, with the intention of never returning, when the doctor comes in accompanied by two male nurses.

The doctor announces, "Mr. Nottingham, there has been a change of plans. You're progressing quicker than we expected. We want to begin therapy sooner rather than later. Nothing major, we just want to see how well you do trying to stand up. Are you feeling up to it?"

"Sure, I feel better today than I have. Let's go."

"Great!" He instructs the male nurses to position themselves at the corners of the right side of his bed. They take down the guardrail and wait for Lance to move. Arizona, still seated in the chair next to his bed, is plotting her escape.

Lance turns his body, and one leg at a time, moves into a sitting position. The two nurses follow his movement closely but never touch him. Arizona comments, "This is a drastic change from just a few nights ago. Pretty soon you'll be able to go home."

Lance responds, "Tell me about it; when I first woke up everything hurt and I could hardly move at all."

The nurses move closer, preparing to assist if necessary. But inch by inch, Lance scoots off the bed, getting ready to stand. While his back is facing her, Arizona notices how his broad shoulders complement his arms. This lively side of him is who she had wanted to meet ever since arriving here. When he turns around to smile proudly, she examines his face. The same way she does each night while he is asleep, becoming even more familiar with his features: the way his long, narrow nose points at the tip, how his eyes crinkle when he smiles and those salmon-pink lips. Both feet are placed on the ground and Lance summons what strength he has, using the bed and his hands to propel him up. The two nurses grip him between his elbows and armpits. As he continues to stand, his legs begin to shake, and after a short while, they buckle as he plops on the bed.

The doctor makes a note in his chart, saying, "Excellent, keep that up and you'll be walking out of here in no time."

Lance beams a smile in Arizona's direction.

The doctor asks, "How do you feel, any pain or sensations?"

Lance positions himself back in bed and answers, "A little tingling sensation in my legs, but other than that, I'm good."

"Tingling in your legs?"

Lance nods.

"That's a good sign. We can try again tomorrow and take it from there."

The doctor addresses Arizona. "Have you brought any mementos?"

"His wallet," she replies, digging through her purse for it.

"Great, keep me updated on any progress you make, Lance."

He and the two nurses walk out, shutting the door behind them. Arizona places the wallet on the bed beside him.

"I look funny," he comments, examining his license photo.

She looks at him, puzzled. To her, he is quite handsome both in real life and in the picture. "How so?"

"You know how when you hear yourself in a recording, you don't sound like you think you do? Well, I guess the same principle applies. It's like looking at a picture of someone you have never met and realizing it is you." He reads the information on his license. DOB 5/30, *30 years old*, Weight 180 lb., Address 4815 Oceanside Dr., Eyes Blue. "It's all here, all the information you told me."

"I spent much of my free time looking at it. It helped shed some light on who you are."

"You really feel that way? This doesn't tell me anything," he said. "There are no real answers on this plastic card or in this wallet." He puts the license back in the wallet, folding it shut. "What I need isn't in there. To tell you the truth, I don't have an identity, I don't know who I am or who Lance is and

I'm not going to discover that by looking in a wallet." He wrapped himself in his emotions like a blanket on a cold day.

In the same way that misery loves company, Arizona feels compelled to stay and help him through this. Reaching for his hand, she holds it in her own and softly strokes it with her thumb.

Closing his eyes, he breathes in and huffs out hot air at first, then coming back to himself, he breathes quietly. *Can two broken halves make a whole? No, but for now, each other's misshapen piece is all they have.* Arizona's locket, which is resting on her heart, catches the light, and Lance's eyes are drawn to it. Her eyes follow his.

With her free hand, she fondles it lovingly. "My grandmother gave it to me for my eighteenth birthday. Whenever I wear it, I'm reminded of her. She was the mother I never had and the kindest soul I ever knew."

She is close to tears. She does not like talking about herself and especially not about her grandmother. Her vulnerability from before felt like just the tip of where her feelings might lead to. She knows sharing them is a human thing to do. However, she has never learned anything other than to outperform, conceal her emotions, and have shallow conversations. Sharing is a mistake, period.

He read her body language like a pamphlet. "I'm sorry," is all he says. She could not look up, and stares at her hands.

He observes her, thinking deeply. *I don't know what it is about her. Behind her façade of composure, I can see her holding back. She has been controlled and contorted into Humpty Dumpty after his fall and I do not know how to help her. I do not even know how to help myself. Behind the pain is a child that's been reprimanded one too many times and is afraid. This is a textbook case of disappointed parents' syndrome; when you fail to please those who are important in your life and navigate through life with a defeated mindset. I know she knows more than what she is telling me, but my fear is that she will never open up. This girl has my answers, but will she let me in to find them?* His thoughts shift. *I know I am Lance, but who is that person? It is hard to picture a version of myself other than the one in this hospital bed. The only consolation in this situation is that this version of me knows her; a gentle soul who saved a dying man in an alleyway. She stayed with me, a stranger in the literal sense, lying for me, yet being completely honest with me. She has the sweetest soul. People like her get hurt easily. Tonight, she is making an effort to be vulnerable. Let me not crush a flower struggling to bloom. Let me embrace her with compassion as she has with me. I cannot help her be whole, and she cannot help me heal, and yet here we are in these fleeting moments. I do not know who I was, but who I am does not know who he is without her.*

She collects her thoughts. Still looking down, she mutters, "Love thy neighbor as thy self." Her head flicks up and she is finally able to look at him.

"What did you say?" he asks.

"Love thy neighbor as thy self," she continues. "I've had the same dream night after night since you woke up. And it always ends the same, with that phrase."

He listens intently and asks, "What happens in your dream?"

She recounts it for him, adding, "I recognized you as my neighbor, because the dream is about what happened to us. That's when the voice from my dream came to me and said, 'Love thy neighbor as thyself.' I had repeated it as a reflex, realizing that you are my neighbor."

"Often times, dreams are a way of putting perspective on the irrational events in one's life," Lance commented.

"Is it hard to grasp, waking out of a coma, nearly dying, and the fact that I found you after having a mental breakdown?" she asks.

"Do you believe that this is more than a random series of events? Do you remember any other sayings like this from your dreams?"

At this very moment, all she can think about is the conversation from the cafeteria. *Everything happens for a reason.* Wanting to understand him, she blurts out honestly, "Are you trying to say this is fate or destiny that our meeting was written in the stars? Is that what you're saying this is?"

"I believe so, don't you? Explain to me how someone randomly finds someone else hidden beneath mounds of trash, finds the help they need to load him into a car, and gets me here just in time to not only survive but have minimal damage. If that doesn't indicate this was meant to happen, then I don't know how to convince you otherwise."

There was a long pause, as Lance's words sink in.

"Get up," Arizona demands.

"What?!"

"I have something to show you. Since you're so big on this fate idea, let me show you what fate really is."

With Arizona's help, he is able to get himself into a wheelchair. She pushes him down the hall and around the corner. They reach a hallway with one full wall of windows looking out at the city's lights and hospital rooms on the opposite side. She parks him facing the door to one of the rooms.

"The person in this room was hit by a car the night I found you. She is in a coma just like you were only, she still has not woken up. If we are tied together by fate, then she is somehow tied together with us. What do you have to say about that?"

Excitedly, Lance suggests, "Let's meet her."

Bewildered by his response, Arizona says, "Beg pardon…?"

"Come on, let's go."

"No!"

"Why not? You said it yourself, we're all tied together. Comas are not so common that two people would fall into one on the same day, in the same hospital. I have to at least see her."

She sighs heavily in surrender. Moving past him to the door, she knocks lightly. When no one replies, she opens the door and pushes Lance inside. The only light in the room comes from a side lamp and a curtain blocks their view of the bed. Arizona maneuvers Lance around the curtain, doing her best not to disturb anything. Lance sits in his wheelchair, perched at the foot of the hospital bed, and Arizona stands behind him.

In front of them is a girl no older than nineteen. The only sound in the room is the steady beep coming from the monitor. They gaze upon this child, whose blond hair is matted almost to the point of dreads. Lance regrets his decision. This just added to the puzzle to be solved without answering anything.

Arizona is saddened by the sight. She saw her as a girl whose life is yet to begin and cannot due to an unfortunate accident. Instead of lying in this bed, she should be enjoying her first year of college, making friends and memories. Arizona pictures the life this girl is missing out on.

Lance is studying her face to see if she looks familiar. The dim lighting was not enough for him to get a good look. He wheels himself around to the side, moving closer until he is face to face. His gaze moves down the length of her body till his eyes meet Arizona's. Speechless, he wheels his chair out the door, Arizona following behind him. She closes the door, and pushes Lance back to the room. Not one word is spoken until they are back in their usual places, Lance in the bed and Arizona in the chair beside his bed.

Arizona breaks the silence. "What happened back there?"

Solemnly he answers, "Nothing, I have no clue who she is. I don't know how or if she is involved in what's going on."

Lance is lying to Arizona. He knows exactly who she is. He had regained a small bit from that night. She had been in the alleyway with him. He did not recall how they had gotten there, what they had been doing, or what happened that landed them in a hospital. Only that they had been there together and now they were here together. He believes even more than before that fate is real and Arizona is more than just a stranger that saved his life.

Lance changes the subject. "Love thy neighbor as thy self, huh; what made you think of that?"

She thinks back to what they had been talking about prior to their field trip. "I was just thinking about my eighteenth birthday. Then I remembered my dream."

"How did one lead to the other?" Lance presses.

"You're not the first person I've taken care of in a hospital bed. My grandmother was…" she pauses to collect her thoughts. "On my eighteenth birthday, I closed my eyes to blow out my candles and make a wish, and when I opened them, my grandmother was on the floor clutching her heart. I called 911." She wipes a single tear from her cheek. "I didn't lose her that day, but came very close to." Tears trickle from her eyes, and she rushes to swipe them away. She giggles nervously, trying to lighten the mood. "Sorry, I shouldn't be talking about such a depressing topic."

"Hey, it's okay. You loved her, there's nothing wrong with that."

Arizona had forgotten about wanting to leave the hospital with the recent excitement, but now she's ready to.

Picking up on her shift in mood, Lance demands, "Tell me your other dreams."

"What other dreams are you talking about?"

Lance does not know about any other dreams, of course, but he suspects that if she left, he would lose her permanently. He would say anything to keep her here even one minute longer.

"You mean to tell me that was the only dream you've had? Have you had any more dreams about us?" Lance waggles his eyebrows and flashes a big grin.

"Not really, and certainly not like *that*."

Stalling for time, Lance digs further. "How about any interesting dreams from before we met. Was there a voice in any of your other dreams?"

His prompting leads Arizona to recall a dream that stirred her very soul.

"Wait, there was one, a while back."

"What was it about?"

"It starts off with me in a skiff in the middle of an ocean or sea. There is a storm raging about me. Thunder, lightning, waves rocking the boat. I was so scared."

"Oh wow, then what happened?" Lance is genuinely interested. Arizona has a gift for storytelling.

"I found something else to focus on and thought I saw a lighthouse. The sight of it comforted me and I even had the courage to walk towards it on top of the water. The waves ceased their raging under my feet. Closer and closer, I trudged to the lighthouse. The nearer I got, the more at peace I felt, and more victorious."

"That sounds wonderful," he comments, fully engaged in her story.

"Yea, it was until I got close enough to realize I was not walking towards a lighthouse. I was walking towards…God. In shock, I lost focus and whatever was holding my feet above the water gave way, and I started to sink."

Lance stares wide eyed as he waits for her to say more. When she does not continue, he prompts her, "Then what happened?"

"The dream ended, and I woke up."

Lance dissects her story in his mind. *If her dreams are telling a story about what is happening in her life, then based on what she just told me, she is struggling with her faith. Whether I call it fate or she calls it God, she must believe that we have a purpose together.*

All the while, Arizona is questioning her personal beliefs. *I have been dancing around the idea of a higher power and now I'm done. Our earlier conversation, all these incidents, and now Lance's insistence on fate; it's all too much. Everything happens for a reason, but who orchestrates what happens? My grandma taught me about God way back when and now it must be my time to choose whether to explore what he is doing in my life today or run from it.*

"You have a gift for storytelling," Lance remarks.

"Do I? Thanks, I guess I don't really use it enough to notice."

"You should, I haven't heard anything that interesting since last week's telenovela." This makes Arizona chuckle. "Please tell me another dream or story or anything."

She looks at the time. "It is getting kind of late. I think I should go."

"Please stay. I'm ten times better when you are around; don't go."

No one likes having me around; I'm not that pleasant of a person. "I really must go," she protests.

"Just a little longer," Lance pleads.

"You and I could both use some rest, we have had our adventure for today."

"I don't want you to go. You are my only friend. Having you here makes being here better; you make me better."

Taken aback by his tender words, her icy walls begin to melt, and reluctantly, she agrees to stay just a while longer.

They do not talk much after that. There is a classic black and white movie on and they watch in silence. Only neither of them is really watching it. Both are miles away, thinking thoughts that should be spoken out loud to each other. Just as the movie is about to end, two nurses come by.

"Is it PT time again? Alright, I know what to do."

One of the nurses lowers the guardrail and stays at one end at the side of his bed. The other stands at the other end, following Lance's feet in case he has complications. This time he stands for longer than before and even manages to take a step.

"See, you're my healing charm," he says to Arizona. At that moment, his legs collapse. The nurse swoops to catch him. "I'm fine, all is good." Lance takes a seat. "I did well, better than before." Both nurses nod their head in agreement at his progress. One nurse lifts his legs back onto the bed and massages them to promote blood circulation. The other nurse exits after Lance is securely in bed. Once the brief massage is over, the second nurse exits and then it is just the two of them again in a silent room.

Arizona is standing by the window, looking up into the sky. Night has fallen, and she is hoping to catch a star or two peeking through the rolling night clouds. "No stars tonight."

"Is that what you are always looking at when you stand by the window?"

"Mostly, sometimes I watch people enter the hospital, sometimes I look off into the distance." She looks at the clock again. "I really must go. I have a long drive ahead of me."

"Leaving so soon?"

She would have left hours ago had she not foolishly agreed to extend her visit. "I have spent my fair share of time here. It's time for me to leave."

"Before you go, can I ask you a question?"

Please no; I have made a fool of myself enough tonight. Let my silence speak volumes and my pleading eyes quiet all curiosity. She shrugs, looking away.

He proceeds. "There's one hundred trillion plus stars in the sky, which one do you look at?" He smiles.

She does not smile back but is relieved that he did not ask anything too personal.

"I try to find Ursa Major and Minor. When the stars illuminate the darkened sky, I can always count on the dippers to shine for me."

"You're into constellations?"

"I am into perspective, imagination, reflection, whatever you want to call it. The stars help me with that. Looking at them helps me think, plus they are gorgeous to look at."

He takes it all in and breathes out, "One more question?"

She sighs internally, the weight of her own thoughts toppling her as he speaks. She realizes he is not going to let her leave. *There will always be one more question, one more reason to get me to stay.*

"Will you be back tomorrow?"

She freezes, unsure of how to answer. She does not have a reason to come back. Never did in the first place other than her curiosity. Ultimately, the question he just asked her is one she has been asking herself.

"You don't need me here," she finally says.

"You really think that?"

"Yes!"

"Well, I think I needed you before I knew you. Look at me Arizona, I'm not that corpse in your back seat. I am alive, and healing. But the journey is not over yet. My memories, my identity have been wiped clean. The only thing I have is you, someone to help me get through this."

He scoots over, making room for her again. Only this time he did not pat the spot for her to join. He lets his heart speak in conjunction with his words. "As much as I want to ask you to stay, and as much as I want to see you tomorrow, and every day after, I won't ask anymore; the choice is yours. Do what you feel is right."

Both hearts beat fervently, each knowing that their future hinges on a single decision. He waits for her. His gaze holds her in place. Trapped in a pool of blue, she could not think. Decisions are not her forte. Her thoughts are racing around at the speed of light. *I thought I was done. Find out if he lives, that's all this was ever supposed to be. I cannot do this. Staying would only complicate my life more. I don't mind being alone. My isolation keeps me safe and no one can hurt me. I've trusted before and been jerked around by so many people. I cannot trust again. He is the same, people don't change. I'm the only one that has my best interest at heart and I have to do what I know is right.*

He can sense her decision and knows how this is going to play out. Arizona is hurting. She has locked herself into isolation and no amount of words can break through. What she needs is something more than words, more than action, or even time. *I cannot help her alone, maybe not even at all, but I know this is fate. I believe that this journey to my memory, towards wholeness, is meant for both of us. This is right, we were meant to meet each other. We need each other. I just need her to see that.*

He is pushing her out of her comfort zone and has been ever since they met. That is the foundation of their relationship. Just as Arizona's composure—the only thing she has been able to maintain—is about to crack, she says the only thing that feels appropriate, nothing. She leaves in silence, walking past his hospital bed, his desires, and his hold on her. The person she is around Lance has been allowed freedom for far too long. Reality needs to set in before this fantasy takes over her life.

Pausing at the elevator, she does not yet know if she is coming back, and she is also unsure of her decision to leave. Instead of getting on the elevator, she wanders around the hospital trying to think. Her memory flashes back to the beginning, the alleyway. That night ended with her purging tears and disappointment. Hoarding her hurt is all she knows and after shedding some it during her time with Lance, she needs to decide if she is going to continue to nourish the pain, or her soul. *I was in it 'ready or not', right? But this is more than what I imagined, too much more. Is this not the very thing that I wanted?* She thinks back to El Dorado and the high hopes she had for that night. *That night, I ended up sulking in an alleyway crying buckets and dying of anxiety because I tried to be happy. But I did something and found someone that is changing my life for the better. Never have I felt free like that before. I was always bound by living up to expectations— the world's, my boss's, my own—and never being able to measure up.*

I could go back. I could walk into the room and sit and stay but... if this ends badly, I don't think I could recover. That alley was a prelude to Pandora's Box. If this attempt for a better life fails, then there is no hope for me, and I cannot live without hope. It's been the only thing keeping me above water. Kurt hurt me, but also taught me a lesson. Staying here would be me ignoring the rationality that my struggles have built inside me. I cannot be shattered into a thousand pieces again and built back up. There is not enough of me left to rebuild anymore. I've lost bits of myself here and there; what's left is all I have. She wanders around aimlessly until she is tired of being inside the hospital. Her feet are sure of the direction they are walking. She gets into her car and drives away. *How do I love my neighbor when I don't even know how to love myself?* She had shown compassion towards a dying soul and Lance had done the same.

PART 3

L ance watches her walk away, his expression crestfallen. He wants to believe she will turn around, that she will change her mind, but she keeps walking, and then she is gone. He does not believe this is the end, but that is what it looks like and he can certainly feel her absence. Even so, he is determined to wait for her. If she changes her mind, Lance will be here with open arms and a loving heart. Arizona may not see the value of their journey or their friendship but Lance does.

Tonight, sleep eludes him. With so many thoughts darting through his mind, he reflects, incredulous, on the events that transpired. *One minute she was here and now it is just me. I don't know if I actually expected her to leave but I have strong hopes that she will return.*

A phrase rings in his ears, as light as dandelion seeds blowing in the wind. He cannot call to mind where it is from. He finally stops trying to remember and meditates on its application to his current state. As soft as before, he hears the phrase again: The substance of things hoped for and the evidence of things not seen.[4]

Lance recalls Arizona at the window from previous nights, gazing out. Last night she confessed that nothing came to her while looking at the stars, and why should it? She had accomplished, without their help, what she thought she could not. She had the answers to those looming questions within

---

[4] Hebrews 11:1

her, all along. *Tonight, it is my turn to look up*, he thinks, although he believes his answers rest in time and chance. He hopes to gain peace, the kind Arizona receives, from looking above. He cautiously adjusts himself so that he is sitting up at the edge of the bed, except this time, on the opposite side. He lifts himself up to a standing position, with nothing else supporting him. *Hey, I'm getting kind of good at this.* His weight is more manageable for his legs to bear. He turns so that he is facing the bed and sits in the chair. His perception shifts to her usual viewpoint. The only thing missing, the most important thing, is him; the impaired man in bed. *I cannot believe she watched over me, night after night, looking at me, knowing I was not just sleeping but in a coma. I cannot imagine what that was like for her.* He surveils the room, catching his breath. Once done, his arms push up on the arm rests, and he lifts himself up onto his feet. Lance feels his body working against him. Sliding one foot at a time, he walks over to the window. He leans against the wall to stay up.

Looking out, he barely sees the moon hiding behind clouds. Trying to capture Arizona's mindset, he begins to think about 'The Beyond' but cannot think past the night he woke up to see Arizona. *The night I first saw her with her curly, wild hair, she looked like an angel with the moon shining on her. Until she turned around and her eyes were bulging out of their sockets. To say she was shocked to see the eyes of a man who had come out of a coma, is an understatement. I wonder if she ever thought I would come to? When she rushed to give me water to drink, that was nice of her. My throat was so parched. If I had tried to talk, it would have cracked open like winter lips.* That memory is strong enough to pull him out of his daydream. *This is a bad idea. What am I trying to accomplish by doing this?*

A red light catches his attention below. He looks down at the parking lot, watching as a white Durango drives away. She chose to leave, and only time would reveal if she would choose to come back. Having failed at finding peace above, he counts all the cars in the parking lot that he could see from his window. Fifty-three. Then he groups them by color: nine red, five blue, fifteen white, ten gray, two green, nine black, one orange, and two yellow. He continues to perform math equations in his head. After cars no longer entertain him, he looks up once more and scoffs at the sky. No amount of imagination could replace seeing the real thing.

Moving away from the wall, he presses on toward the bed, but his legs give out and he falls, hitting the ground hip first, his hands instinctively covering his face and head. Pain resonates throughout his body. *Oooouuuch!* is his first thought. After a few minutes, the pain subsides enough for his second thought. *I need her, and she left me.* And then, *The substance of things hoped for and the evidence of things not seen.* Feeling pathetic, he blurts out, "What the heck is the substance of things hoped for and the evidence of things not seen?"

"Faith," a deep, African-accented voice shouts from above.

A brown face peers over the bed at Lance lying on the floor. "Is anything broken? I am going to help you up, is that okay?" With wide, round eyes, the man looks down at the fallen Lance, asking him, "How did you end up down there?" Reaching out his hands, he grabbed him around the waist. Lifting him up, he sets Lance on his feet, helping him walk him to the bed. He sets Lance down then proceeds with more questions. "Are you experiencing any pain? Do I need to get a nurse?"

Lance takes a second to determine if his body is in unbearable pain anywhere. "I should be fine. The only thing truly hurt is my ego."

"What are you in here for?" asks the man. Before Lance could answer, the man grabs his chart and reads the information he's looking for out loud.

"Admitted by orphaned sister, multiple surgeries, coma, memory loss. Recovery plan: physical therapy." Looking up from the chart, he says, "Yes, I see. It is a miracle that you were up in the first place, let alone starting PT so soon. You are in good shape. Why were you asking about faith earlier?"

"Was I? I didn't know what that phrase was referring to or where it came from. I just kept hearing it in my head."

"And you had no prior conversations about faith before then?"

"No, I was just hoping that something would happen and then the phrase just popped into my head."

"This is looking very good for you my friend. Your miraculous healing, hearing about faith. Do you own a Bible?" Before Lance could answer, the man pulls one out from the nightstand on the side of the bed. "Here, flip to Hebrews."

Lance stares at the book in his hands, confused, while the man pulls out his mini Bible and flips through the pages until he is near the back of the book. He shows Lance the page. "Hebrews, chapter eleven, verse one."

Lance skims the words. *Now faith is,* then he recites the rest of the verse out loud, "...the substance of things hoped for, the evidence of things not seen." Understanding washes over him, then confusion. "How do you know this scripture and how do I?"

"Has something just happened that caused you to go off course?" the man asked Lance. "If so, I think He is giving it to you to hear. Your faith needs to be rooted in the correct source and greater than your doubts."

"What does that even mean? Who is giving me this?"

The man gives a hearty laugh that fills the room. "You ask a lot of questions whose answers must be sought from the correct source." He points to the Bible and continues. "What else have you been hearing?"

Lance thinks back to Arizona's dream. "Love thy neighbor as thyself?" His answer is immediate, with a smile that pushes his cheeks up to his eyes. "Jesus said to love thy neighbor as thyself. This is the second of the commandments. The first is to love the Lord thy God with all thy heart, soul, and mind."[5]

Lance ponders on this. *Before Arizona left, she was talking about the internal struggle with her faith. Maybe I have been thinking about this all wrong. Could it be that my purpose is to help her? But not towards wholeness, at least not by my own efforts, but to lead her towards God and let him do the rest?*

The man says, "Is that all?"

Lance now feels he is meant to meet this man and talk about the Bible. *Nothing happens by coincidence. There is a bigger picture*, chimes in his head. He then realizes that what is meant to happen is happening right before his eyes. "Could you hear me yelling from the hallway, is that what prompted you to come in?"

The man first places a cup of water on his nightstand next to the Bible he'd pulled out of his pocket. Then he answers, "I was sent to deliver things."

---

[5] St Matthew 22:37-38

Lance starts to ask him something else but stops. He already knows the answer. The man turns to walk away, but then Lance exclaims, "Hey, you forgot your Bible."

"I meant to, she'll need it."

Lance is thoroughly perplexed. *Surely, he could not be talking about Arizona.* "I never caught your name."

"I never said it," the man states, before turning and rushing out the door.

Lance pushes off and rolls out of bed. Using every surface available, he maneuvers himself to the door. The wheelchair is still there for him, so he squats then sits in the chair and wheels himself down the hall. In his pursuit for answers, he weaves around people as they stroll along. By this time, the man is way ahead of him, but Lance's laser-beam eyes hold a steady focus on him. The man turns a corner. Lance pushes onward. After rounding the corner, he stops, trying to locate the man. Lance wheels a few feet forward then hears a familiar voice in the next room.

"It may look bad now, but that's how things work. Weeping may endure for a night, but joy comes in the morning.[6] Your morning will come just you wait and see."

Lance wheels himself to the doorway as the source of the voice and shadow move behind a curtain. The shadow pushes back the curtain revealing a girl in bed. The man waves Lance inside. Lance strains his ears to hear him now, although moments ago his voice was audible from the hallway.

"I like to visit certain patients. I think hearing a familiar voice helps."

---

[6] Psalms 30:5

Lance's silence signals his assent. He comments, "She was admitted almost a month ago." Lance wheels himself next to her bedside. An earlier glimpse of a memory had revealed that they were together in the alleyway. *What were we doing there?* Lance studies her. *I don't understand how you got mixed into this mess. I'm aware that I can do nothing but watch and wait. You are so pale, so young, too young to experience this. Too precious to be here and too loved to remain like this.*

The man speaks as he plumps the girl's pillow. "I struggle sometimes with the things I see in this hospital. Although I see death on a regular basis, I know miracles can and do happen. My hope is not in what I see, but in what I know. For what a man seeth, why doth he yet hope for? Hope that is seen is not hope. But if we hope for that we see not, then do we with patience wait for it."[7] He moves around the bed tucking in the blanket, securing it under the mattress. "You've not said a word—has your voice run away with your memories?"

Lance smiles, appreciating his lighthearted teasing. The steady beeping of the heart monitor fills the silence.

He directs his next words towards the girl. "My friend, Lance is here visiting with me. Let me introduce you to him so he can stop being shy. Lance, this is Odessa."

The name resonates in his ears as his memory flashes back to midday in the alley. Her smiling face appears briefly and Lance can picture her wearing a red cap, tattered shirt and ripped pants. She is sitting on the ground, resting in the alleyway against the same brick wall that had held him up when Arizona discovered him. He whispers involuntarily, "Odessa." At the sound of his voice, the monitor beeping increases.

---

[7] Romans 8:24-25

"What just happened?"

Lance clears his throat. "A piece of my memory..."

The man cuts Lance off, absorbed by the sudden spikes in the lines on the monitor. "Look! Something is happening. The beeps are louder and faster. I'm going to get help." The man hastily leaves for the nurse's station.

Lance continues to talk to the girl. "Odessa, I remember. Not everything, but I remember you. You look different without the hat covering your hair. We were together in that alleyway." He pauses to let the words sink in and then asks, "How did we end up here?" He rests his hand on her arm. At the touch of her skin, memories flash and fade. A tall man, a darkening sky, a red hat fading into the distance, then nothing.

A team of nurses and attendants surrounds her bed. Lance is pushed out of the room by someone in scrubs and taken down the hall back to his room. He watches the flood of memories playing across his consciousness, oblivious of anything else tonight. He is unaware of the exact time he got to his room or how long he has been in his bed. Snapping back to the present, he is overcome with exhaustion. With his back pressed to the mattress and the sheets wrapped around him, his eyelids droop and blink at decreasing intervals until they shut for the night.

As the sun comes into view over the horizon and soars upwards, so do Lance's eyelids. He awakens with more than the understanding of what the substance of things hoped for and the evidence of things unseen is, but with Faith itself. He begins his day by picking up the Bible and searching through Hebrews. He reads through the first three verses of the first chapter, then skims through the next several chapters until he reaches Hebrews 11:1. "Now faith is the substance of things hoped for, the evidence of things not seen." He pauses to meditate on what the verse is saying, trying to encapsulate the entire meaning into his mind. Lance then returns to the page. "For by it the elders obtained a good report. Through faith we understand that the worlds were framed by the word of God, so that the things which are seen were not made of things which do appear."[8] He has to stop and deliberate again. This continues until he finishes the entire chapter, which includes names of people he did not know about and refers to acts he has not read yet. Lance may not understand what he has read but he understands that if one has faith, the highly unlikely becomes possible. Once the word nourishes his soul, he thinks long and hard about last night.

Lance tries his best not to think about Arizona but that is where his mind takes him first. *She should be sitting in her seat next to me; we should be reading the Bible together. Brokenness cannot heal itself, only God can.* Lance does not fully comprehend the journey he is embarking on, but he knows that his begins with faith and Arizona's journey begins with love.

He persists in thinking about Arizona, hoping she is okay and clinging to the belief that she will return. She saved his life and now he feels it is his turn to repay the debt. He began this process expecting to help make her whole. Now, he sees that is for God to do and Him alone. When she returns, he needs to be ready to guide her, especially if she is prone to running when challenged. He wants her to trust the journey towards God, and not the momentary complacency of running from him.

Around twelve o'clock, the doctor and two nurses show up to continue physical therapy. Similar to before, Lance swings his legs over the bed, this time with more ease. The nurses

---

[8] Hebrews 11:2-3

assume their positions on either side of him just in case. He places his hands on the bed directly next to his legs and with flat palms, pushes off the edge and stands solid. Lance's feet grip the cold tile floors. This time, there are no wobbly ankles or weak knees. The doctor waves for Lance to walk to him. He peels one foot off the cold tile and the other follows. In four steps, he reaches the doctor successfully.

The doctor congratulates Lance on his success. "You must have discovered some secret potion. Your mobility has improved, literally, overnight." He records Lance's progress and then tests him further. "Can you shift your weight onto your left leg, and now your right?"

Lance sways left then right with ease. The doctor jots down more notes, then instructs him further. "Can you bend your knees?" Lance starts to squat, then whoosh—he heads for the floor. He would have hit the ground had the nurses not been there to catch him, each with a hand under his armpits lifting him up. Lance returns to the bed.

Once he is alone, he gets the urge to read more. He picks the Bible up and randomly flips through it. Lance finds a few interesting scriptures but the one that has the greatest impact on him is 2 Corinthians 12:9. "And he said unto me, My grace is sufficient for thee: for my strength is made perfect in weakness. Most gladly therefore will I rather glory in my infirmities, that the power of Christ may rest upon me."

If any doubts exist in his mind that it is the Lord's place to fix someone, they are erased with this verse. Picking out verses encourages him. He flips through and looks at the entirety of books within the holy book. At the back is some additional information. He stumbles upon the concordance to the Old and New Testaments and looks specifically for "faith", skimming through the noted verses. Then he finds the listing for "love" and starts at the beginning verse. Leviticus 19:18 stands out. "Thou shalt love thy neighbor as thyself." He notices that same phrase in Matthew 19:19, 22:39, Galatians 5:14, and James 2:8. *There are too many verses to look at in one sitting; where do I begin?* The antiseptic air seeps into his lungs, and he impatiently pushes it out. He wants to pray, but is unsure of how to have this conversation out loud.

"How do I start? God, I hope Arizona is okay, and thank you for sending her as an angel to save my life. Little did she know you have a plan to bring her back to you. Little did both of us know I would be the person to help with that task. Please protect her wherever she is."

He ends his prayer with "Amen" then gets up to go visit Odessa with the Bible still in his hand. His mobility is improving but he still needs to stay close to the wall when progressing down the hall and around the corner.

As Lance's hand pats against the wallpaper, his thoughts meander alongside him. *God has awakened me from a coma only for my memory to be locked away, and for Odessa to be the key to unlocking them. I know she has something to do with me being here, but if my last memory is of her red hat fleeing, then how did she end up here? Oh Odessa, how did you get mixed into this?*

The door to Odessa's room is cracked open, and standing before the threshold, Lance strains his ears to hear the familiar voice inside. He pushes open the door to find the same man from the night before sitting with Odessa's hand cupped between his two. Lance's presence did not disturb them. He hears the man's words clearly. "Give us this day our daily bread. And forgive us our debts, as we forgive our debtors. And lead us not into temptation, but deliver us from evil: For thine is the kingdom, and the power, and the glory, for ever.

Amen.[9] Wait on the Lord my child and be of good courage."[10] He places her hand on the bed, stands, and turns to walk away, finding Lance standing in the doorway.

The man, unfazed by Lance's unexpected presence, notices he is not in a wheelchair, and remarks, "You seem to be doing much better. Have you come for me or her?"

Lance silently points to the girl in the bed.

"I thought as much. Here, come sit." The man helps Lance as he walks towards the chair. One cautious step at a time they move, until Lance is sitting down. The man's voice hovers behind him. "You know, last night, her monitor beeped the strongest since she was admitted. Her vitals have been low, but steady. For the first time, we all had hope. Her care is being covered through State insurance. She doesn't have any family. Nineteen years old and she has no one to look after her. She has a few more days, maybe a week. She is blessed to have had the length of time that she did. But just pray my brother. Pray the will of the Lord." With a single pat on his shoulder, the man turns to walk away and disappears.

Lance is left alone with Odessa. The weight of the news crushes him. In the light of day, he can see her clearly, although, in her current state, he wishes he could not. He wants to say something that will make this mountain of a problem better, however, he knows his words cannot provide the help that she needs. With this in mind, he pulls out the Bible from the nightstand and reads God's words. Lance wants to let God know that he is counting on Him to work a miracle. He wants to say that in prayer, but when Lance opens his mouth, he breathes in and the only word that comes out is, "God!" He

---

[9] St. Matthew 6:9-13
[10] Psalms 27:14

admires the prayer of the man who occupied this chair before him, going before God with boldness. He sighs. Lance feels uncomfortable about praying, but he prays anyways. Even if the words he speaks are not elegant, God knows his heart.

Where to begin? Lance flips through the Bible searching for the perfect passage. In the process, he discovers a verse not for Odessa but for himself. He begins to read St. Matthew 17:20. "If ye have faith as a grain of mustard seed, ye shall say unto this mountain, Remove hence to yonder place; and it shall remove; and nothing shall be impossible unto you." This pricks him in his heart. *Faith can move mountains*. He reflects on what Faith is. *The substance of things hoped for, the evidence of things not seen*. He also thinks about the mustard seed, somehow recalling it is one of the smallest of seeds. He compares the size of the seed to the amount of hope he should have in the "substance". What is the substance? *Substance, substance*. Abruptly, a revelation strikes like lightning. *The substance is God, God is my substance! I cannot do anything on my own. It is Him alone who orchestrates all of this and it is he who will pull Odessa out. My Faith is in Him to perform the miracle, not in the miracle itself.*

He slumps down in the chair, the revelation hitting him harder than the news about Odessa. Basking in his realization, a sound begins to come through to him. The monitor is beeping insistently, even stronger than last night. He remembers touching her hand and gaining a portion of his memory. He wonders if he touches her hand again, whether the same thing will happen. Desperately, he wants this to work. He hesitates, his hand hovering inches above hers. With a single breath, he prepares for the flood of memories, then closes the gap an inch at a time. When no memories emerge, he opens his eyes and looks around sheepishly. Recognizing that they are not in some science fiction movie, he lets out the breath he has been holding, pats her hand, and smiles. Lance sits with her in silence, letting the moment settle. He gets up to walk back to his room. Before leaving, he remarks, "You know, I have never left this room with less than what I came here with."

He returns the Bible to the nightstand and departs. Just as he had yesterday, he leaves with another piece of the puzzle and the sound of her monitor's steady beeping playing in the background. Lance is hopeful that this means she will wake up soon.

Walking back to his room, his legs start getting a little wobbly. Still, he presses on knowing it's just down the hall. Left foot in front of right, one knee bends a little, and then the other. He uses the wall for support. Lance does not see any benches to rest on or mobility aids, however, everything seems to be working fine until he reaches the occupied hospital rooms. *Of course, all the doors would be open.* The first few doorways are cake to walk past, but as he keeps going, he leans on the wall more and more. The openings are hard to maneuver around, but he presses onward. His strategy is to push off the wall near the doorframe and let gravity, as well as his hand-eye coordination do the rest. Everything is going well until he reaches the room before his own. Somewhere between pushing off the doorframe and reaching the other side, he misses. The air whisks around him as his body plummets towards the cold tiles. Hands flailing, his chest hits the ground forcing the air out of his lungs. His head, unprotected, hits the ground next, *crack.* The last image he sees is of the dimming florescent lights as the blackness overtakes his consciousness.

Lance heaves as he trudges forward. The sun's merciless rays shine as the beads of sweat trickle down his back making the white shirt that sticks to his skin translucent. Dry spots form in the back of his throat. He keeps swallowing as a temporary fix. He treks on despite the uncomfortable conditions. He looks ahead up the mountain. Accompanying him is the pre-memory-loss version of himself. The self he believes knows no sorrow and lives a life of carelessness.

"Hey friend," pre-memory-loss Lance calls, "is there any water left?" Lance chucks the bag at him. Just a trickle of water touches his tongue.

His pre-memory-loss self does not recognize the Lance of today. Each has a life apart from one another, separate thoughts and different aspirations. Yet, today they travel together for a single purpose.

Pre-memory-loss Lance carries a sack upon his back with wood, the other carries a box of matches and a rope tied to a lamb. Their lungs protest with each arid, exasperated breath. For the majority of the trip, not a word is spoken, only the sounds of grunts and crunching gravel can be heard. In a barely audible voice, pre-memory-loss Lance chokes out, "How much longer?"

Lance announces, "Just up ahead, it should not be long now."

"All this, just to sacrifice a lamb?"

The Lord has given Lance a purpose, separate from his former self, and he is walking in it; however, a small part of himself is in pursuit of something more—his memories. Lance is at the point in his journey where he will be given his next steps. He must show that he is ready for it by denying his will, picking up the cross, and fully living the purpose God has placed over his life. This pilgrimage is that very test. He answers, "This sacrificial journey is about more than killing a lamb. It's showing God that we are able to kill our personal pursuits in order to fulfill his will."

"What are you talking abo…" pre-memory-loss Lance begins, before Lance interrupts.

"Keep up. I can see the spot up ahead." They arrive and find a wooden bed and nothing else.

"This is it? This is what we came all this way for, a bed of clay and a place for wood underneath?"

"Load the wood," Lance directs. "I will prepare the sacrifice."

Pre-memory-loss Lance loads the wood under the bed, one log at a time, for the sacrifice. Lance, knowing what has to be done, unclips the lamb and pushes him away, freeing it.

"What are you doing? That was the sacrifice!"

"No, it's not. God wants a different sacrifice." Lance moves closer to pre-memory-loss Lance.

"What are you talking about? What else have you to give?"

Lance explains. "I have been trying to find myself, a person that does not exist anymore. That is who needs to be sacrificed."

"If he doesn't exist, how can you sacrifice him?"

"He does exist, and he is who will be sacrificed."

Pre-memory-loss Lance says nothing, but squints at his God-fearing counterpart.

"He is here." Lance lunges at pre-memory-loss Lance, screaming, "He is you!"

Lance restrains his companion's wrist, while tackling him to the ground. They wrestle; gripping, twisting, kicking, rolling around on the ground, while dust flies. Pre-memory-loss Lance, in an attempt to become free, pushes Lance away giving himself enough time to grab a handful of dust. Pre-memory-loss Lance throws it in Lance's eyes. Lance protests, his eyes clenched shut, one hand franticly wiping at the debris. His other hand is still tightly gripping pre-memory-loss Lance's wrist, even tighter now. Captive Lance pushes and kicks at his attacker, to no avail. With strength like Samson, Lance snaps pre-memory-loss Lance's wrist, breaking it. Pre-memory-loss Lance screams. Instinctually, his good hand reaches toward the pain in his other wrist. Falling to his knees, he cries out in agony. Finally, the sacrifice is subdued, and bound by the rope which once held the lamb. Lance places his other self on the altar. Knife in hand, he raises his arm up high.

As he is about to plunge the knife into his heart, a voice stops him saying, "Lay not thine hand upon the lad.[11] Except a man be born of water and of the Spirit, he cannot enter into the kingdom of God."[12]

A second voice says, "Repent, and be baptized every one of you in the name of Jesus Christ for the remission of sins, and ye shall receive the gift of the Holy Ghost."[13]

Lance shouts at the air, "Is this not what you wanted, Lord?" Just then, a pool of water appears. He runs towards it jumping in; his whole body is submerged.

After a moment, he pops up and opens his eyes. No longer wet or in a desert, he is now staring face-to-face into the eyes of a familiar friend—Arizona.

Lance plops his upper half back down onto the bed, still reeling from his dream. He closes his eyes, taking deep breaths. His hands gather at his face, rubbing his eyes.

"Intense dream." Arizona's voice speaks softly from the direction of the window.

---

[11] Genesis 22:12
[12] St. John 3:5
[13] Acts 2:38

Startled, he snaps his head toward the voice realizing he is not alone like he thought. Lance relaxes and perks up once he confirms who it is. "It was vivid to say the least!"

"That's how it works. At least for me that is how it works. When I dreamt I saved a stranger from dying, it was as if I were actually there."

Lance smiles broadly. "What are you doing here?"

"The hospital called to let me know you had an accident."

"And you came?"

"Yes, I wanted to make sure you were okay."

"And if I wasn't, Arizona? What if I was not okay, huh? How would your presence here help?"

"I suppose it wouldn't help. Wow, this is a drastic change. I thought you would have a different response."

"Arizona, you really hurt me by leaving. I know you thought you were helping but you cannot just exit and enter into someone's life, like you're walking through a door."

"If you want me to go, I'll leave. I probably should not have come back to begin with." She stands, prepared to leave, but stops when Lance continues.

"I'm not telling you to leave. I just want you to be honest about why you came back."

"Lance, we've been through so much together. Why wouldn't I come if something happened to you? The night I brought you here, I made a promise to myself that I would see this through."

"Then why did you leave in the first place?"

"I knew I could leave and you would be okay." Arizona surveys his body. "Looking at you, healthy and healing, I convinced myself that it was over."

"The night you left, I thought that meant it was over and that terrified me. But here you are. And now I'm scared that you'll leave again. Can you imagine the only person you know and trust with your life leaving?"

"I thought things would be better if I left. Me being here complicated things. I thought I'd be okay walking away."

In a soft voice, Lance replies, "If you believed that then honestly, why did you come back?"

Tell him Arizona, say it. Say, I left you before you left me. There is a long pause. "I was scared you wouldn't want me here once you healed completely." Arizona looks up. Closing her eyes, she sighs.

"I was afraid of the person I was becoming when I was with you. I was losing the self I've always known." A tear crawls down her cheek as she speaks truthfully. "But I came back because I don't like her. She's angry, and hurting, and dying. And she's killing me."

That is all he needs to hear. Getting out of bed, Lance wraps his arms around her. Arizona's face is buried in his chest and her tears pour unto his hospital gown. He does not say a word. He just embraces Arizona, and she lets him. They stay like this until Arizona's crying turns to sobs. He pulls his upper half away to see her better, still holding her in his arms.

"I want you to read something with me," he says. She takes a seat on the bed. Lance heads to the nightstand and grabs the Bible meant for her, along with some tissues. He sits on the bed next to her. Flipping to 1 John 4:18, he tells her, "I don't want you to be scared about what God has in store for you. I know it will be hard, that it's *been* hard, but things will get better. You just have to trust the process."

He reads, "There is no fear in love; but perfect love casteth out fear: because fear hath torment. He that feareth is not made perfect in love." He pauses to let the words sink in.

"That was not just for you but for me as well. The night you left, I began to think about faith. I later discovered what faith actually is. My faith has to be bigger than my fear. Once I knew where to look," he adds, holding up the Bible in his hands, "everything became clear. I understand who my faith should be in and where my faith is leading me. Arizona, let God's perfect love cast out your every fear."

If she had any tears left in her, they would have run down her face. "You sound like my grandmother. She used to read to me from the Bible when I was little."

Arizona takes the Bible in her own hands. The sensation of the leather against the palms of her hands and the thin pages reminds her of the meadow behind Grandma's house. Arizona smiles, recalling a particular day when the tall grass danced in the summer breeze. Her smile makes Lance smile, and he waits until she is ready to share. After a few precious moments she speaks.

"I remember this kind of Bible; it reminds me of when I was little. During the summer, my grandma would pack a basket for our trips to the meadow behind her house. They would be full of sandwiches, chips, something to drink, and chocolate-chip cookies. The cookies were my favorite. She and I would make them from scratch and save them for our outings to the meadow. Even to this day, chocolate-chip cookies take me back to the meadow. She would pack a blanket for us to sit on. Grandmother would carry that, while I carried two Bibles— one for her and one for me. In the meadow, we ate our meal and afterwards she would read to me. Sometimes we would even look up at the clouds and laugh at the funny shapes and images we saw. Thinking back, I can still see the purple wildflowers surrounding us."

Coming back to reality from her memory, Arizona sees Lance, enthralled by her words, his sympathetic eyes focusing on her face.

"That sounds beautiful. Your grandmother sounds like a wonderful lady."

"Oh, she was. God fearing and all. You know, she raised me to be like that but when she passed, I lost my way." Arizona looks down at her hands, comprehending how dysfunctional her life has become. "I loved her so much and when she left, it was as if pieces of me went with her. I was never the same; even now I am still not the same." Arizona admits, "I am broken, I am hurting, and I need help. The night I saved you, I was at my breaking point. I was hoping for a change in my life, but was seeking it in the wrong places and that night I wandered into an alley and cried. I cried until I did not have a single tear to shed. When I stumbled upon you, my first thought was to help you. Once I did that, I stayed hoping you were the change I needed. I felt stupid for believing you were my answer. I didn't want to be disappointed again, not after getting my hopes up. I left, and I didn't plan on returning. I left intending to live my melancholy life."

She stops momentarily, building courage within herself to admit out loud a self-evident truth. "But I couldn't. I became fed up with my life. I realized I was running, from you, from my faith, from a better future. I don't want to run anymore. I'm done barely living life. I want to experience fullness of joy. I want to be whole."

He takes her hand in his. She looks up, meeting his gaze.

"I am glad you came back Arizona, because, I think I have the answer. Do you remember when I first woke up from my dream?" She nods her head. "Well, at the end of the dream, I heard, 'Repent and be baptized every one of you in the name of Jesus Christ for the remission of sins, and ye shall receive the gift of the Holy Ghost.'"

Skeptical, she asks, "How is baptism the answer?"

"Because God says it is. My faith is in him, and I believe that if God gave it to me as the answer, it's the answer for you too."

Incredulous, she replies, "How would something God told you to do help me?"

"He sent you to save me, so that I can send you to him, and he can save us both. Baptism is our admittance to him that we cannot save ourselves. Only he can and did on the cross when he died for our sins. God has already saved us, we just have to—for lack of a better term—be initiated via baptism."

"Wait, how do you know all of this?"

"I have been reading my Bible and talking to a man in the hospital. He has been helping me navigate through things. I don't know who he is, but God knows who to send to help us out. God has tested my faith multiple times and each time I've answered with 'Speak; for thy servant heareth.'"[14]

"I think you hit your head a little too hard, maybe you should lie back down."

Just as Lance begins explaining about the man, the man comes running into the room and rests against the door frame. He rests for three long deep breaths, then calls out to make sure he has Lance's full attention.

"What is going on?" Lance asks.

---

[14] 1 Samuel 3:10

S. Chapman

"You must come quickly, it's Odessa. She is awake!"

CHAPTER III

Instantly, Lance flings his legs over the side of the bed ready to hit the ground running to reach Odessa, then stops himself. Pulling his focus back to the present surroundings, Lance turns towards Arizona. As he looks into her almond-shaped, hazel eyes, he realizes he has to explain some things to her before he can go see Odessa. Lance turns towards his friend who is panting in the doorway.

"Is she stable?" Lance asks.

"She is causing quite the commotion, but she is holding steady as far as I can tell."

"How long has she been awake?"

"I don't know. I was heading to her room to pray and heard screaming and I noticed nurses and doctors running in. Running into the room myself, I saw with my own eyes that, sure enough, it's true. She has awakened. I do not know her state of being. I ran straight here to tell you."

Lance takes the man's words in like air and releases his own, "If you wouldn't mind, please watch over Odessa until I am able to get to her."

In disbelief, the man responds, "You're not coming?"

"I'll be right there. I'll go to her, but I need a minute before I do."

He nods his head, looking past Lance. "Oh, I see." Then he walks back out into the hallway.

Lance stands up, testing his strength.

Arizona asks, "Odessa—is that the name of the girl we visited, the one who was brought here the same night as you?"

Lance sighs as he answers the question, "That's correct."

The volume of her voice decreases. "You figured out her name?"

The silence takes over as he struggles to begin his explanation.

Arizona prompts him, "It wasn't written on her charts; hospital staff could not find it in any previous records. Yet, you know it? How Lance, how did you figure it out?"

Lance turns to face her, finally ready to explain things. He speaks slowly, battling to find each right word as the previous one escapes. "I know her somehow. We know each other very well, actually. When we first entered her room and I saw her, it triggered a memory." His speech begins to flow, less choppy and overthought as he tells her what he remembers. "I believe we were in the same alley where you found me. I saw her sitting on the ground, resting her back on the wall. She wore a red hat. My next memory was of her retreating into the distance."

Arizona silently takes this in. Her gaze remains focused on the blankets. His words are painted along the walls of her mind. *Red hat, alleyway, they're friends.* Once her brain processes everything she returns her focus to him.

Lance patiently waits for her to say something, anything. He wants to cut the tension with a smile. His hand wants to rest on hers as if to say "We are still in this together." He wants to tell her "I am here with you, I am still here for you." More than anything that he wants to do and say, his greatest desire is for her not to leave again.

She parts her lips and words break the silence, "I know you did not have to share that with me, so thank you."

Lance, relieved at the direction of the conversation, continues. "I wanted to be completely honest with you and I wanted to share what has happened while you were gone…"

"But…" she starts to interrupt, but Lance stops her.

"I want you to understand—because of what I now know, things have to change."

Thoughtful, she stated, "I don't understand."

He looks away recalling everything he used to want. "I wanted to know who Lance was. When we were looking at his picture, it did not feel like that was me. All the information seemed to point to someone else. I felt so disconnected from someone who everyone thought I was supposed to be. When I looked in the mirror, I saw his face but it was not his anymore—it was mine. I thought I needed my memories back to help me figure out who I was. But that's just it. Who I was is not, and never will be, who I am today. Odessa was my key to unlocking what I thought I wanted to know, the memories of a dead man. I understand now and am hesitant to visit because a part of me wants those old memories but more of me doesn't. I have a new mission and it is doing what God told me to do."

He corrects himself with a smile and with such honesty in his eyes that any reservation she has vanishes. "What God told *us* to do."

She looks at him, understanding what comes next, reciting, "Love thy neighbor as thyself, love the Lord, and walk in uncompromising faith."

"That sounds about right," he answers. "Okay, what happens for us next is…"

She raises her eyebrows skeptically.

Seeing her facial expression, he clarifies, "Yes, we are in this together. God has given me our next steps and it has everything to do with my dream."

"How are you so sure this is what God wants for the both of us?"

"Because it's what he wants for everyone. It's biblical." Lance's excitement begins to spring forth as he directs her to the Bible. "Look." With the Bible in his hand, he franticly flips through until he reaches Acts 2:38. "Here, 'Then Peter said unto them, Repent, and be baptized every one of you in the name of Jesus Christ for the remission of sins, and ye shall receive the gift of the Holy Ghost.'" He flips over to Saint John 3:5 and continues reading. "'Verily, verily, I say unto thee, Except a man be born of water and of the Spirit, he cannot enter into the kingdom of God.' And before that it says, 'Except a man be born again, he cannot see the kingdom of God.'[15] It's right here in red ink, it's what I saw in my dream. I believe this is what we are supposed to do next."

She looks at him with concern and stares into eyes that echo the heart of God's words. Her own expression softens, and she places her right hand on his left and says, "Ready or not, I'm in."

He smiles, overjoyed. He removes his hand and implores, "Come on, let's go get baptized."

"Wait, where is there enough water in a hospital for a baptism?"

"That's a good question." He thinks about it and then says, "I have no idea, but my friend will know." Lance is convinced that his friend knows the answer to everything. "Let's go find him."

"What do you mean, find him? Shouldn't he be watching over Odessa?"

---

[15] St. John 3:3

Lances answers her as they walk down the hall side by side. "Truthfully, I don't think he is. He always seems to be near when I need him. Despite where I asked him to be, he could be anywhere."

"Then where are we going if he could be anywhere?"

"We are taking a stroll around the hospital. If I don't know where a large tub of water is, and my friend with the answers is not in sight, then maybe we will stumble upon one or the other."

They walk down one hall, and turn into another, not heading towards any destination in particular. As their conversation develops, Arizona says, "I feel like you've gotten so much out of me while I don't know a thing about what you've been going through."

"What do you mean?" he asks.

"I guess you seem really composed about this whole ordeal. I never realized the extent of what you were going though, having lost your memory."

"What brought on this question?"

"Earlier, when you were explaining, you said you wanted to know who Lance was and that he didn't feel like you. I never thought of you as two people; Lance was always—you. Yet to you, he is another person? I guess I am curious about that."

"Um, let me see if I can explain it." He recalls his feelings and tries to articulate them. "When I first woke up, I wasn't thinking about my name, or the first time I rode a bike, or even the last person I talked to, which are things Lance would know. But the moment I opened my eyes, that's when my life started. My memories began then. I wasn't worried about where any of my *friends* were," he said, making air quotes with his fingers. He turns to Arizona, smiling. "You were there. I

106

wasn't worried about my health. I was alive, and painfully sore, but breathing and in a hospital full of people who took an oath to keep me alive. Initially, I was okay with my situation, but soon after I started to question everything I didn't know. I felt like I was missing something. There I was feeling incomplete and wanting to know who I was before the accident." He thinks a bit and restarts. "Gaining my memories back seemed like the right thing to do. You know, the next step; it seemed like the cure to my situation. I felt like having those would solve everything." Squinting his eyes, he looks up as if to search his brain to make sure he has gotten everything out. "Did I explain that well? I feel like I was all over the place."

He tries to read her face, as she interprets everything he revealed about his situation. Finally, she answers him with a question.

"Do you still want to know about the incident that brought you to the hospital?"

He thinks about that for a minute before answering. "Yeess," he says, cautiously dragging out the word before explaining further. "I do, but I am no longer trying to gain my memories back in order to find out."

"Right, but don't you think Odessa could help with that? If she doesn't have memory loss and has calmed down enough to have a conversation then she would be able to help connect the dots about that night."

With less enthusiasm than she would have guessed, he answers, "I suppose."

Taking note, she comments, "Wow, I wasn't expecting that response." They walk silently until Arizona probes further. "I thought you wanted to know what happened that night."

"I do, but…" He hesitated before confessing, "I'm afraid that will trigger more memories."

"Wouldn't that kind of be the point?"

"Yes, but I don't want to change back. I don't want the memories to trigger and bring the old Lance back. The more I know, the more I change; and I like me, and I love this godly pursuit I'm on."

Grabbing his hand in solidarity, she interjects. "You mean *we're* on. Don't forget you have me here. I like the new Lance too. If I truly thought this would compromise the progress God has made in your life, I wouldn't have suggested it."

Arizona breathes in the overly cleansed air. "You are currently who you intend to be forever, right? Gaining old memories won't change that. You'll just have more of the story of how your life transformed."

He thinks about that. "You're right. I shouldn't fear my past or my future when God is in it. But I am just so scared that if I know who I used to be, I'll become him, and lose myself— kind of like Dr. Jekyll turning into Mr. Hyde."

"You have to know that the memories themselves will not change you, your reactions to them will."

"But, what if my mind…" His thoughts trail off and he drops the idea. Before Arizona can address this, he picks up a new thought. "Please help me not to change back."

"I don't think that is how it works, but what if the old you *was* good?"

He momentarily stops her from walking further. Looking deep into her eyes, he pleads, "It doesn't matter. He is not me and I don't want to be him."

"Fair enough," she responds before looking away.

He squeezes her hand lightly. She looks at him. He speaks in softer tones. "Hey, I didn't mean to be so abrupt, but we don't know what's going to happen. I just..." Again, he struggles for words then finds new ones. "Losing my memories is the blessing that helped me become the person I am supposed to be. God worked it out so that I have you, I have purpose, and a future rooted in Him. I don't need much more than that and I don't need my memories."

"I understand you don't need them, but you cannot run from them. God has not given you a spirit of fear, but of power, love and a sound mind."[16]

He sighs, knowing she is right. "Wait, what happened here? Did I get schooled just now?"

She chuckles, seeing firsthand how similar they are in what they need. "I think I get it. I get why you need faith and I need love."

Lance retorts, "I have faith!"

Arizona snaps back, "Not if you don't believe He can keep you who you are even with your old memories."

She smiles, signaling this is a playful moment although her words ring true in his ears. "You cannot just believe in God, you must also believe in God's ability to help in all situations."

He looks at her with wide eyes, shocked at her emphatic declaration of faith. But he likes it and suddenly grins.

"What?!" she exclaims, happy he has taken on the same mood as she.

"It's just nice to see you like this."

"Like what?"

---

[16] 2 Timothy 1:7

"Happy."

Arizona looks down, hiding her smile because for the first time in a long time, she *was* happy. She turns to face Lance when he keeps talking.

"Things have changed so much for us both since we first met. That's partly why I wanted to take some time and let you know what's happened. I mean, we are in this together and I didn't want to hold anything back from you."

"I appreciate that," she says.

They walk in silence for several moments, stealing glances at each other and beaming. One would give the other's hand a playful squeeze and the other would give one right back. Arizona is the first to break the silence.

"You know, your eyes are like two pools that someone could drown in if you stare at them long enough."

"I wouldn't want to drown anyone, but if we could use them to get baptized in that'd be mighty helpful."

Arizona rephrases what he said, "Baptized in a pool. That's it! Baptized in a pool. Why didn't we think of this before?" She knows exactly where to go. She pulls him along as she searches for some type of directory or sign that would point them to the right area.

He allows her to direct him. Confused, he asks, "What just happened?"

"I just figured out where we can go. Sometimes, when expectant mothers give birth, they want to use a birthing pool. I believe its standard for larger hospitals to have at least one."

"Oh, that's a good idea."

He picks up the pace, realizing what they are doing. They dart from hallway to hallway searching for a sign of some sort to indicate which floor Maternity is on. When they cannot locate one, they approach a desk behind which staff are moving about efficiently.

"Excuse me," Arizona says in greeting. They continue their activities. She tries again, a little louder, "Pardon me."

Again, no one looks up from their tasks.

This time, she yells, "Code blue!" causing five heads to pop up, ten eyes staring at her.

Now that she has their attention, she asks, "Where is the Maternity center?"

"Follow the signs on the seventh floor," one of them replies. Arizona thanks her. As they were leaving, the staff member adds, "Miss, next time you want our attention, just ring the bell."

Arizona and Lance glance down to see a shiny, golden call bell and a sign that says "Ring for assistance". The staff return to work and they walk towards the elevators.

Once on the seventh floor, they casually stroll to the desk and this time, they tap the bell, getting the attention of a very nice nurse. "May I help you?"

"Can you tell me where the birthing pool is?"

"Is there a special reason you need to go there?"

Arizona had not anticipated any questions. She figures now is a good time for her storytelling skills to come into play. Before she can tell her tall tale, Lance's friend comes strolling around the corner.

"Hey Lance, Arizona," he calls.

The nurse questions the man, "You know them?"

"Yes, Lance awoke from a coma not too long ago. He was having trouble walking so I suggested water therapy. Arizona is listed as family."

The nurse scrutinizes Lance and declares, "He looks to be walking fine to me."

Lance's friend agrees, stating, "Yeah, he has come a long way, but to reduce his pain I would strongly recommend he try it. I want to see him off the pain medication he is currently taking. If you don't mind, I'll take over from here."

Before the nurse could object, the man says, "Have a good one."

"You too," the nurse calls to him as the three of them continue down the hall.

Once out of sight, Arizona feels comfortable enough to ask, "How did you know...?" She could not decide how to end her question since she could be referring to any number of things. So, she leaves it at that.

He answers, "Right place, right time." He smiles at Lance and asks him, "Isn't that right, Lance?"

"Happens every time," Lance agrees then adds, "You get used to it."

Lance's friend asks, "I assume you need the birthing pool for a good reason?"

"Yeah, we want to get baptized," Lance says. "I'm sure you can help us with that, right?"

"Of course I can help with that. I have performed many baptisms."

The three of them walk until they arrive at a room with a large tub that resembles a jetted hot tub. Lance and his friend start preparing the birthing pool. Arizona observes them working.

"Wait, wait, wait a minute." They stop to look at her. "How does this work?"

Lance takes a stab at answering. "Well, we get in and completely submerge ourselves under water." Lance looks to his friend for confirmation, who takes his cue and explains further.

"Pretty much, although before you go under, a prayer is said, and you are baptized in the name of Jesus. Afterward, you will tarry for the Holy Ghost."

Arizona, squinting her eyes, asks, "Tarry? For the holy *what*?"

"Technically, there are two types of baptisms: one of water and the other of spirit. Tarrying is the second part and it's how you receive his spirit. I know it is a foreign concept but the Holy Ghost is explained throughout the New Testament. Here, I'll show you."

He pulls out the Bible from his back pocket and turns to Acts 1:5.

"'For John truly baptized with water; but ye shall be baptized with the Holy Ghost...'"

He then flips to Matthew 3:11 and reads it to her. "'I indeed baptize you with water unto repentance: but he that cometh after me is mightier than I... he shall baptize you with the Holy Ghost and with fire.' Verses about tongues are found in Acts 2:3-4." He finds the verses and reads, "'And there appeared unto them cloven tongues like as of fire, and it sat upon each of them. And they were filled with the Holy Ghost, and began to speak with other tongues, as the Spirit gave them utterance.'

"There is also Acts 2:38." He recites it from memory. "'Repent, and be baptized every one of you in the name of Jesus Christ for the remission of sins, and ye shall receive the gift of the Holy Ghost.' I know this is unlike anything you have experienced. I understand if this is something you need more time to think about. Hebrews 6:1-2 states that before baptism, one should repent from dead works, and have faith in God. If you've taken those steps and if baptism is something you want, then the only thing left is for it to happen."

Already in the pool, Lance calls out to his friend, "It's all ready to go and so am I."

He nods to Lance and finishes up with Arizona. "Jesus was baptized himself[17] because he knew that's what had to be done. He is the perfect example for us in every way. He began his earthly ministry with baptism and the Holy Spirit, which is interchangeable with the Holy Ghost. I will urge you not to get in the water if you do not intend to live wholly for God or if you're not ready for God to alter your life in a radical way. I can only confess that it is the single best decision I've ever made. With a glad heart, I can truly confess, 'As for me and my house, we will serve the Lord.'" With sincerity in his voice, he explains further.[18] "The Holy Ghost is the way you and God communicate. It is personal, and may feel weird at first, but like any language it starts off with baby babble, then transforms with practice into full-blown sentences that are sent to God. I'll be ready for you whenever you decide to carry on." He hands her the Bible and prepares himself next to the pool to baptize Lance who is fully enjoying the warmth.

Once in position, he kneels beside the pool with one hand on Lance's shoulder and the other raised in reverence to God. Instructing Lance, he says, "I am going to pray first then you must be completely submerged in the water. Afterwards, there's more prayer till you speak in tongues. Now, tongues look different for each person. For some, they come out of the water speaking, for others it takes hours or even days. Some

---

[17] St. Matthew 3:16
[18] Joshua 24:15

114

get hot; some add motion, like running, or jumping. Some speak for hours, some minutes. It is a very personal process; do not get discouraged if it doesn't happen right away."

"Sounds good, chief, I am ready."

Lance is sure of what he is about to do. He is fully confident that this is the next step he needs to take to fulfill God's will for his life. Lance's friend begins the baptism with a prayer.

"My dearly beloved brother, Lance Mason Nottingham, upon the confession of your faith in the death, burial, and resurrection of the Lord Jesus Christ, and in the confidence which we have in the blessed word of God, I now baptize you in the name of the Lord Jesus Christ for the remission of your sins; and ye shall receive the gift of the Holy Ghost. Amen." He gives Lance's shoulder a slight push downward, signaling to him that he should go under.

Arizona watches, her thoughts circling on her next move. *To be baptized or not to be baptized —that is the question.* Everything that is happening is good, Arizona cannot deny that. She wants to be made whole, and happy, and if this is how that happens then so be it. She is all in. Part of her wonders if this is the answer to her life's dilemma. *Lance seems so sure and rightfully so. He has been given signs and dreams. He is advancing. I want to do this but is what I truly want worth what I am about to go through?* she wonders, quickly forgetting that she has also received those very things. Lance's perceived spiritual advancement is the direct result of living out what God has given him and investing time to learn more about God through his word.

She watches them. Paying special attention to Lance, she recognizes how great his change has been from nearly dying to abundantly happy and healthy. Her thoughts take over. *Wasn't that me? Nearly dying, rotting from the inside out.* Just then, she recalls part of a verse, Psalms 30:5. "Weeping may endure for a night." Her heart begins to tremble knowing this verse can be applied to her situation in the very alleyway where she found Lance. She turns to 1 John 4:18, the scripture she and Lance looked at earlier. She reads it and then proceeds to read beyond it to verse 19. Slowly, her eyes probe each word. Her heart is pierced with truth. "'We love him, because he first loved us.'" The words "he first loved us" resonate in her heart. "God is love."[19] A few tears escape from her eye, trickling down her cheek. She does not bother to wipe them away. She just lets God's word ring true as his love works to penetrate her heart. At the very second Lance goes under, she knows exactly what she is going to do.

Swiftly she gets up and carefully turns the doorknob and sneaks out not wanting to disturb what is happening. She walks down the hall. Arizona ducks into empty rooms looking for a particular type of clothing. She assumes she'll find them in a drawer or maybe hanging up somewhere. Finally, she happens upon a supply closet where, after doing some digging, she finds exactly what she is looking for—an extra pair of hospital scrubs. After disrobing, Arizona puts on the top and pants. She folds her clothes and with them neatly in hand, she walks back to the birthing room.

Ready to begin, she sets her clothes down. She can hear Lance more than she can see him. It is just like the man said. Lance is speaking in an unfamiliar language; to Arizona it sounds like gibberish. She scans the room and sees the other man praising God by the pool. Patiently, he waits for her just like he said he would. She makes her way to the pool. Looking for Lance again, she finds him in a corner practically hidden

---

[19] I John 4:8

by hospital machinery. Now that she has watched the process, it is time for her to experience it. She reminds herself, *There is no fear in love; but perfect love casteth out fear.*[20] As she recites this in her mind, she lets His love pour over her, and surrenders all fear and doubt. The man begins, she is submerged in the water, and she remembers that Christ first loved her. Arizona comes up and is immediately handed a towel. The man helps her out of the pool and they tarry for the Holy Ghost. They are standing in the middle of the room, away from Lance and the equipment.

"Before we begin, can you close your eyes and take a deep breath in and release."

She does as he instructs. Her lungs fill with air, then slowly she releases it.

"Great," he says. "Now keep breathing, in and out."

She hugs the towel closer as time goes on. After several minutes, she comments, "I don't think this is working, I don't think I'm any closer to receiving the Holy Spirit then when I started."

He calmly states, "That is not the purpose of this particular process."

"Then why are you having me do these breathing exercises?" she retorts.

"For you to relax; you seem very tense. I believe when one is not so wound up it makes the process easier."

She breathes, and then shoots him a friendly smile as she wraps the towel around herself and tucks the end in. She then twists her body from side to side, loosening up. She wiggles

---

[20] 1 John 4:18

her shoulders in circles and says, "I think I'm pretty relaxed now. Let's do this."

He puts his hands on her shoulders and applies a slight pressure to push them down.

He smiles. "Now, let's do this. When you feel ready, just say hallelujah."

He begins by praying over her. Her brain absorbs the prayer and she can picture the words in her mind.

Eyes closed and heart open, she begins to say hallelujah. Slowly at first, then he instructs her to say it faster. Still praying, he prompts her to say it faster. She tries, but becomes quiet. He instructs her to open her mouth. She wants to but cannot. It is as if something within her will literally not let her open up. Finally, she fights to open her mouth and no sound comes out. She pictures the words he is saying in her mind, and then other words come to her, gibberish, but she cannot get them out either. He keeps praying over her and five minutes turn into ten, then into fifteen, and eventually they reach the half-hour mark. He stops praying and talks to her. She opens her eyes.

Lance is sitting in the chair holding her clothes in his lap. He watches them, waiting for a good moment to interrupt.

The man asks Arizona, "What's going on?"

Flabbergasted, she responds, "I don't know."

"What are you thinking about?"

"The words you are saying, God's love, scriptures. I can see the words, but my voice won't work properly. It's like something inside of me is broken. At one point I could not even open my mouth."

He looks at her puzzled, then asks, "Okay, would you like to try again?"

"Yes."

He looks at her for a beat, then at Lance and instructs her to change into her regular clothes. She walks over to Lance who hands her the clothes and whispers to her what God told him to tell her. Lance announces out loud that he is going to give them some privacy and head to Odessa's room. Lance's friend nods his head. Arizona, whose hand is already on the doorknob, opens it up and walks towards an empty room so she can change. Lance follows her. Arizona looks back at the door of the birthing room. Lance grabs her shoulders and pulls her close. They wobble a little but remain close. Arizona maneuvers her arm, reaching around his waist. He does not care that she is still somewhat wet. They simply hold each other silently as they walk.

She thinks about what he whispered to her moments ago. "It takes **faith** and **love**. One is not superior to the other; they are partners working in tandem. Don't rely on one to compensate for the other." She knows he was talking about qualities, yet she wants to believe he meant the two of them as well. Soon she finds a room and pulls apart from Lance. He lets go and they split up. She changes silently, folding the wet clothes and leaving them in the bathroom sink when she is done. Arizona heads back to the birthing room ready to try again. Lance, having already completed his next step, receives what he needs from God to continue on this mission of completeness. He heads to the elevators on his way to Odessa.

As Lance approaches Odessa's door, he cannot help but notice his lack of uneasiness. His stomach does not churn, no nerves-induced perspiration accumulates—nothing. He does however feel a peace about this, one that surpasses all understanding.[21] Lance is at the stage where he not only believes in God, but believes God can do all things, for those that love him and who are the called according to his purpose.[22] He walks into the room knowing that this is God's will. He used to be afraid to know who he was. Lance thought his past would stop him from being who he currently is. But now, he realizes when God works it out, it is always for the better.

Lance confidently approaches Odessa's bed, knowing that regaining his memories will not change him but will add to his perspective on this situation. The message he heard from God is the driving force behind his understanding, and ultimately led him into this room. *If I don't remember what I've been through, I will never know how great my testimony is. I won't know what God has brought me through.*

Lance briefly thinks about the verses God gave him from the Gospel of Luke. In Luke 7:38-48, God educates Simon the Pharisee and a woman with a parable about debtors. Afterwards, God explains why the woman washes His feet with her tears, dries them with her hair and gives Him many kisses, and why Simon does not. It is because her many sins are forgiven. God tells Simon, "To whom little is forgiven, the same loveth little."[23] It is because of God that Lance can stand here unashamed and unafraid of who he was before. God knows who Lance used to be and his sins are forgiven. This is Lance's chance to discover just how far God has brought him. For Lance to continue on this journey, his faith must outweigh his fear.

---

[21] Philippians 4:7
[22] Romans 8:28
[23] St. Luke 7:47

Lance walks closer. He sees Odessa perk up as he walks closer. Her mouth never moves, but the expression on her face supplies the confirmation he was hoping for. Old Lance was a good person. Still, neither of them say a word. He takes a seat next to her bed and waits for her to speak. Her eyes follow as he moves closer. Once he is in place she addresses him.

In a raspy voice she mumbles, "It's good to see a familiar face. I woke up to a hundred faces and yours is the first one I know."

"It's good to see you, too, Odessa. You look different without your hat. I almost did not recognize you."

She turns away from Lance.

"Odessa, are you okay?"

"You don't remember do you?"

With a furrowed brow he asks, "Remember what?"

"Anything—I know you don't. There is no sense in pretending on my account."

"How...?" He realizes before completing his question that his friend had done more than watch over her.

She continues. "There was a man here. He did not tell me his name, but he had a unique accent. He told me that you were here and that you would come to see me soon."

Lance did not bother to ask how his friend knew that the dots would connect or that she would remember and want to see him. "He told you everything?"

"Everything I needed to hear."

"Like what?"

"When I first woke up, I was in such a panic as all these people came in and then even more. They flooded my room and I felt trapped. When I tried to get away, they restrained me. I was screaming and thrashing, and they wanted to inject me with something to calm me down. I saw the syringe and began to fight even harder. They injected me, and I calmed down. They ran some tests and talked amongst themselves. I didn't understand most of what was said to or around me. The man came while they were all still conversing. He convinced them to take a break from testing and to let me get some sleep. When they left, he told me you would come see me, but that you needed my help remembering things. Somehow, I could tell he was telling me the truth. When I saw you come through the door today, his prediction was confirmed."

Curious, Lance questions her. "How so?"

"You always greet me the same way. Every time I see you, without fail. I can always count on you to greet me with a special song."

"Song?" Lance repeats, surprised.

"Yes, you start by asking me if I know what today is. Sometimes I answer by singing the song. If I don't start singing, then you do."

"Me—sing?"

"Yes, you actually have a nice voice in my opinion. I'll start singing it for you. When you remember it, chime in."

Odessa takes a deep breath and clears her throat, and then she begins to sing:

"This is the day, this is the day,

That the Lord has made, that the Lord has made,

I will rejoice, I will rejoice and be glad in it

And be glad in it."

She smiles, hoping something in his head will click. He just stares, wide eyed. It is almost as if he is looking *through* her. She frowns, thinking the singing has not jogged his memory.

When Lance refocuses, he looks at her and his eyes start to tear up without spilling over. "Thank you, Odessa,"

"Did it work?"

"Yes, I remember the song. I remember singing it to you in the alleyway. I can even recall verse two and how on the days you weren't happy, I would keep going till you would sing with me." Lance clears his throat and begins to sing.

"I will enter His court with thanksgiving in my heart.

I will enter His court with praise,

I will say this is the day that the Lord has made,

I will rejoice for He has made me glad."

"That's it. You do remember!" she bellows. They both beam excitedly, overcome with happiness.

Lance says, "A lot of my memories of us consist of this alleyway."

Odessa looks down. Thinking about the alley brings back glimpses of the night they had the accident, the one that landed both of them in comas. She knows eventually she will have to explain to him about that night. Things were so joyous at this moment, and she did not want to dampen the mood, not now. She wonders if this is the right time.

Lance changes the subject. "Can you tell me about how we met each other?"

She smiles at the memory. "You were serving food at a homeless shelter and I walked in hoping there was still food left. You were serving brussels sprouts, my least favorite veggie. When I came to your station, you asked if I would like some." Her smile turns upside down and she pokes her tongue out. "I politely declined. You persisted and said that they were full of nutrients, which a growing person like me needs."

Remembering bits and pieces while she was talking, Lance adds, "And you still declined."

Odessa smiles, raising her eyebrows. "Do you remember what I said?"

He tries to summon up the words she used. Unsure, he says the first thing that comes to him. "You said, 'I think I am done growing'?" As Lance speaks each word, he is surer of it.

"Exactly!" Odessa attempts to regain control over the storytelling. "Then I said…"

But Lance jumps in and they both finished the sentence in unison, "I guess people with red hats are too cool for brussels sprouts." They both laugh at the memory.

Lance leans back in the chair, reliving the memories. His eyes tear up again, this time from laughter. *Arizona was right. I should not fear getting my memories back. I was not a bad person! I volunteered at homeless shelters. I was kind, and from what it sounds like, I knew God before my accident. But that does not explain how we ended up here.* He ponders how to introduce the subject.

Odessa stares at Lance, waiting patiently. Finally, she stretches over and waves her hand in front of his face. "You don't remember the talk we had about how I ended up on the streets, do you?"

He shakes his head.

"One weekend, months ago, I saw you walking downtown by my alleyway. I didn't know where you were headed but when you spotted me across the street with my 'Anything will help, God Bless' sign, you jogged across the street to meet me. We had talked previously at the shelter so we were familiar with each other, but this was the first time I'd seen you away from the shelter. You said, 'Hey Odessa, I saw your hat and knew it was you.' We both laughed and continued with some small talk. Then you heard my stomach grumble and you invited me out to eat. You even let me pick where we would go. I was a little suspicious, but I also hadn't eaten that day. I did not know where to eat, so you said you'd take me to your favorite Mexican spot. We went and before our waitress could take our order, you started praying. I just looked away. At that time, I didn't know what to do and I felt awkward just watching. After we ordered, you were talking about family and your mom and dad; you were very smooth. I still don't know how but you got me talking about my family. I talked about my parents which led me to tell you my story about how I ran away. My father was a very abusive man."

She looks at her hands in embarrassment as she fidgets with the blanket. "He would beat my mom. He broke her arm and a few of her ribs before. I would try to stop him, but he would threaten to beat me too. My mom made sure that she was his only punching bag, but one day she vanished, without a note or clue as to where she went. That is when he started taking his anger out on me. At that point, I had to leave home. I grabbed some money and clothes and got the heck away from him. I started searching for my mother but mostly I was escaping from that horrible man."

Her throat begins to tighten as she tries to hold back streams of tears. Water droplets trickle from her eyes onto her blanket and hands. She wipes them away, but more take their place. "I am so sorry, Lance. I never meant for anything bad to happen."

Lance holds back his questions, listening intently.

She takes slow breaths trying to work through her thoughts and continue. "My dad came looking for me, and found me in that alleyway. He was so angry; I could see pent-up rage in his eyes. If he got ahold of me, I knew he would not only beat me, he would kill me. You were with me, explaining how I needed to get off the streets and that I could have a better future. When I saw him walk up, it felt like my heart stopped beating. You noticed, and immediately realized that was my father. You showed no fear. You whispered to me that you would distract him, and told me to run, and that we would meet up at El Dorado. You told me to take the long way just in case. I wondered what you meant by 'just in case' but was too paralyzed to speak. We both stood up. You walked up to him and before you could say anything, he immediately swung on you. You ducked and yelled at me, 'Run!' and I did. I ran away, while you fought for your life against a man who beat people for fun. I did not look back for fear that he was somehow following me. A few blocks away, I ran into an intersection without paying attention to traffic. A car could not stop in time, and hit me. The next thing I knew, I woke up here and before I could worry about what my father had done to you, your friend showed up and told me you would be coming to see me."

Odessa wept openly, her face tearstained and her sheets soggy from the downpour. Lance could not help beginning to cry a little, hearing all this.

"'Greater love hath no man than this, that a man lay down his life for his friends,'"[24] Lance recites and falls to his knees, worshiping God for His magnificence. *Christ was and is alive in me!* He selflessly sacrificed himself and because of that, he met Arizona, and helped bring her to Christ. Lance realizes a person weathers unpleasantness not only for themselves, but to reach someone else. *Thank you, Jesus! What we endure may not make sense while we're experiencing it. It might not feel*

---

[24] St. John 15:13

126

good and may cost our pride, sanity, or lives, but when we get through it successfully, it's a beautiful situation. Just like Job—after withstanding my ordeal, I have ended up with double what I started with.

Lance declares, "Whatever it takes."

Odessa is staring at Lance, shocked. This is not the reaction she expected.

While Lance is praising the Lord, God reveals another memory to him. This one was of her father standing over him, ready to administer the final blow that would knock him out. He said something, but Lance cannot recall what it was.

Lance finishes, stands up and reaches over to hug Odessa. She continues to stare, befuddled.

"I thought you would be mad at me," she says.

"Mad? Not at all. Thank you, Jesus. Through it all, he knows what he is doing. How could I be mad at you? None of this is your fault."

"But it was my dad who almost killed you and who was the reason we both ended up here."

"It may look like that, but God's grace and mercy was with us through every misadventure we experienced." Lance pauses to look up and praise a little more before continuing. "Listen, everything happens for a reason and if I would have died, so be it. I didn't though, because God reveals situations that seem like certain death to be His divine interworking manifested in our lives. I'm basically Lazarus." He says the last with a lighthearted chuckle. "You didn't do anything. We are both alive, and guess what?"

She looks at him. "What?"

"I made a friend and she just got baptized! If everything we went through helped save another soul, it was worth it. Don't you think?"

She answers with a smile. "Lance, I'm glad you are alive."

He smiles in return and says, "I'm glad we are *both* alive."

At that moment, the doctor and a group of residents come in. Lance is instructed to let Odessa rest and that tomorrow morning is the earliest she'll be allowed visitors. They say their goodbyes and he promises to visit again soon.

As he's leaving to head back to his room, he finally recalls her father's last words to him that night. "You didn't put up nearly as much fight as my late wife did. You pathetic, worthless excuse of a man." Lance cringes at this memory of his final moments before blacking out that night, and the significance of her father's words. But that pales in comparison to the remorse he feels for Odessa and the knowledge he now carries with him, knowing he will have to tell her at the appropriate time.

Lance arrives at his room, his head buzzing with new information. Arizona is lying on his bed and greets him smiling.

"How did it go?" she asks.

"Good, and for you?" he asks, referring to her second attempt at speaking in tongues.

"Not so good. We tried again but no luck," Arizona replies, looking away.

Comprehending her reluctance to continue, Lance changes the subject. "You were right; Old Lance was even better than New Lance."

"Interesting, considering *you are* the old and new Lance," she comments.

"Yeah, I guess I am and always was."

He spends half the evening sharing memories of Odessa, until his eyes grow heavy. Both he and Arizona fall asleep in the hospital bed, close and uncomfortable, but too exhausted to let it bother either of them.

Arizona's mind dances with each story Lance shares, before she enters slumber land. She pictures Lance singing, Odessa and him meeting for the first time, and how gracious he's been to Odessa as he has been to her. She is blessed to have met someone who far exceeds her wants and helps fulfill her needs. She thought she needed a relationship. What she actually needed was companionship—friendship not predicated on how she looks or on being pleasant or perfect. Lance is a God-fearing man who she was able to help in a physical sense and who was able to help her spiritually.

As she enters into REM sleep, her dream, seeming as lively as reality itself, takes her to the meadow. She, Odessa, and Lance are in a flower-covered field. They dance on purple flowers and green grass as the sun kisses their skin. Eventually, they find themselves sitting on the ground, each with their own Bible to read from. It is Arizona's turn to read a passage. "'And when they were come to the place, which is called Calvary, there they crucified him, and the malefactors, one on the right hand, and the other on the left. Then said Jesus, Father, forgive them; for they know not what they do. And they parted his raiment, and cast lots.'"[25] She repeats a portion of the passage, "Father, forgive them, they know not what they do." It plays and replays in her mind. *Forgive them, Father, they know not.*

---

[25] St. Luke 23:33-34

She awakens with those words fresh in her mind. A thought pops into her head. *If love is the key, then forgiveness must be the door that love unlocks.* She lays there for a minute letting the grogginess lift. Once she's relatively alert, she takes a second to observe Lance who is still fast asleep. She carefully extricates herself from the bed and walks to the window but instead of looking up at the stars, she looks off into the distance. She thinks back to the night she found Lance, and compares it to the present. *Faith and love really do work together. Love is the key that unlocks forgiveness, but I need to walk by faith to get through.* She paces in front of the window pondering how faith will help her forgive. *What does the Bible say about this topic?* "Father, forgive them." *Father, forgive me.* She then prays the only prayer she can think of—the one her grandma taught her when she was little.

"'Our Father which art in heaven, Hallowed be thy name. Thy kingdom come. Thy will be done in earth, as it is in heaven. Give us this day our daily bread. And forgive us our debts, as we forgive our debtors. And lead us not into temptation, but deliver us from evil: For thine is the kingdom, and the power, and the glory, for ever. Amen.'"[26]

Still pacing, she repeats the prayer. She closes her eyes as she speaks, opening them only to make sure she is not going to run into anything. She repeats the prayer a third time. Arizona then starts to say hallelujah, rapidly, just as she was instructed after her baptism. Pausing to breathe, she makes sure she is relaxed. She feels a heat come upon her and the hallelujahs come and the heat with it. Her words begin to shift, and she begins to speak with other tongues, as the Spirit gives her utterance.[27] She starts out speaking in hushed tones but as

---

[26] St. Matthew 6:9-13
[27] Acts 2:4

things progress, her volume increases just loud enough to wake Lance. He searches the room for the noise and immediately finds Arizona. A wide grin breaks across his face and he begins to praise God too. She becomes aware that her voice is not alone but she is too in the zone to care. They both succumb to God's almighty power and yield themselves until daybreak.

Physically exhausted, they lie in bed strengthened and encouraged in the Lord, knowing that the provision they need exists in his presence. They are too tired to dream. Yet, after receiving what they needed from the worship session, no dreams are necessary.

Arizona recognizes that a broken and a contrite heart, God will not despise,[28] but He will take away the stony heart out of the flesh and give a heart of flesh[29] in its place. She is no longer clinging to past relationships. She has something better than Kurt or speed dating and feels assured of her future. She has God who is able to do exceeding abundantly above all that she asks or thinks,[30] and He has done so. She offered her damaged heart to Him and he did more than fix it. He showed her how it became broken, how to fix it, and how to guard her new heart. She knows it all happened through baptism, the Holy Spirit, submission and obedience.

---

[28] Psalms 51:17
[29] Ezekiel 36:26
[30] Ephesians 3:20

CHAPTER IV

After three more long weeks of healing, the day when Lance is well enough to leave the hospital finally arrives. Arizona is at the front of the building, waiting by her car as the nurse wheels him out to her. Lance eases into the backseat.

"Hey, how's it feel to be a free man?" someone asks from the passenger seat.

"Odessa, hey, you got your hat back!"

"Not quite, this one's new, can't you tell? It's redder than the last." She smiled playfully then added, "Arizona bought it for me."

"Oh, how could I have been so blind?" he jokes. "At any rate, it looks very nice."

"Thank you."

Arizona hops in the driver's seat and takes off.

Lance takes one last look at the place he spent the past few months in and smiles. *That chapter of my life is now done.* He looks out at the buildings and trees as they pass, enjoying the change in scenery. Absorbed in the world outside, he does not notice where Arizona is taking them until she pulls into the driveway at 4815 Oceanside Drive.

"I know this place," Lance remarks.

"You should, silly, it's your house," Odessa responds and passes him the key Arizona is holding up.

Lance ignores her comment and runs to the front door, unlocks it and rushes in. The ladies follow after him. Lance disappears while Arizona picks up the heaping pile of mail that has been collecting on the floor below the mail slot. Odessa plops down on the couch. Arizona joins her, sorting through the junk, looking for anything important. It was mostly junk mail besides a few past due bills.

The faint sounds of a shower running could be heard from the living room. Odessa gets up to look around. She notices a family photo of Lance and his parents. As she stares at the photo, her heart begins to ache. Odessa is quick to wipe away the tears that threaten to wet her cheeks. It was not until this moment, seeing this family photo, that she had stopped to realize how much she still misses her mother. More tears begin to fall, and before she can escape to another room, Arizona is by her side, pulling Odessa into a loving embrace.

"What's happened?"

Odessa silently sobs on Arizona's shoulder.

"I miss my mom. I haven't seen her since the night she left."

"Do you know where she is?"

"No, she didn't tell me anything. One day I woke up and she was gone." Odessa's sorrow grows from silent sobs to wailing. "She left me with that monster, she just up and took off. She left me."

Arizona lends her shoulder for as long as Odessa needs it, rubbing Odessa's back, letting her release all the pent-up emotion.

Lance walks into the room, sees Odessa crying and mouths to Arizona, "What happened?"

Arizona mouths back, "She misses her mother."

A flashback of the incident with Odessa's dad tries to emerge but Lance dismisses it as a false memory. He walks out of the living room, and then reappears with some tissues, handing them to Arizona, who passes them to Odessa. She blows her nose and wipes her eyes.

Once she calms down, Lance talks to her. "Are you okay, Odessa?"

She nods her head.

"Do you want to talk about what upset you?"

"I really miss my mom. It's always been my mom and me. For her to leave without me...I just don't believe she would."

"What do you think happened to her?" Arizona asks.

"I think she got fed up with being a human punching bag. When the coast was clear, I think she booked it. I just don't understand why she wouldn't take me with her."

"Do you think it was her choice to go?"

"What are you getting at?" Arizona questions him.

"Maybe she didn't have a choice in leaving. Do you think..." His voice trails off as he readjusts the sentence. "Do you remember what happened the night she left?"

Odessa thinks back to that night. "I awoke in the middle of the night to my dad screaming. That was not the first night something like that had happened. I pulled the covers over my head and squeezed my hands to my ears. After twenty minutes, the commotion stopped, and a door slammed shut. I assumed he left, so I went to tend to my mom. She had a black eye and some bruises. She told me to go back to bed. I gave her a hug and a kiss and then went back to bed." Fresh tears begin to flow.

"I remember feeling so bad that this was our life. My mother being beaten by a big bully, and me, living in fear that this would be our lives forever. I wanted better for us. I went back to sleep and didn't hear anything the rest of the night. When I awoke, she was gone, and he was passed out on the couch."

"Huh, is that everything you remember?" Lance asks.

"Yeah, why?" Odessa responds.

136

Without answering her, Lance continues his questioning. "Do you believe your mother would leave you and not tell you or come back to get you?"

"Lance!" Arizona interjects. "Can I talk to you in private?"

The two head to a bedroom in the back of the house. They speak in hushed tones.

"What is going on with you Lance? You are being a real jerk. The girl just misses her mother. Don't you dare make her feel worse than she already does."

"Listen to me Arizona, I think Odessa's mom left, but not of her own free will."

"What are you trying to say, her dad kicked her mom out?"

"No! I think he killed her!"

"Are you serious? Why would you think such a thing?"

"Well, for starters he almost killed me. Also, I think he might have confessed to me that he did."

"Do you have any proof?"

"Nothing other than a memory. That's why I'm trying to see what Odessa can recall about that night on her own."

"You cannot do that to this girl; if she thinks her mother is dead, it will devastate her. The way you're doing it is especially wrong."

"Then what do you propose?"

"Take it to the cops. Let the professionals deal with this, especially if he did do what you think he did."

"That's actually a really good idea. Let's go tell Odessa that the cops are going to…" putting air quotes around his next words, "find her mom."

He walks out of the room and Arizona follows him.

"Odessa, we want to help you find your mom," Lance announces.

"What?!" Arizona exclaims. Odessa looks at them in confusion.

"Correction, we want the cops find your mom," Lance states. "I mean, we do too, but it's better to have an army helping the cause."

Her eyes widen but she says nothing.

Arizona asks, "What do you think of that, sweetie?"

Odessa opens her mouth, but no words come out.

"It's okay if you don't want to, or if you're scared. We just thought this would help," Arizona explains.

Odessa finally answers them. "I want to find my mom, but what if she doesn't want to be found?" Arizona and Lance look at each other. Odessa continues, "Or what if she doesn't want me to find her?"

Arizona swoops to Odessa's side, comforting her. "Oh no, no sweetie, your mother loves you very much. If she's hiding, it's from that brute, not you. I'm sure she wanted to take you with her or tell you."

"Odessa, if you don't want to go to the police, we don't have to, but we think that is our best bet for finding your mom. We can always ask them to be discreet and to make sure that if she is found, her identity will be safe."

Odessa wipes away the remaining tears, grabs them both and hugs them. "You two are the best. Thank you so much."

They drive to the police station; this time Lance is in the front seat and Odessa sits in the back. Lance has a chance to really look at his neighborhood. It is nice, family oriented. There is even a nearby park where children are playing. He imagines that one of the children is his own, and they are playing on the monkey bars and sliding down the slide together. This occupies his thoughts until they reach the police station.

Once they're standing at the front desk, Arizona starts the conversation. "Hello, officer, we would like to file a missing person's report."

"How long have they been missing?"

Odessa speaks up, "A couple months."

Flabbergasted, the officer asks, "Why did you wait so long to file a report? Why now?"

Lance answers. "Long story short, we were in the hospital and unable to make the report until now. Do you think you can help?"

"We'll try, but I need some more information before we can do anything." He grabs a pen and a form and begins questioning her. "Who is the missing person?"

Odessa answers, "My mother, Irene Freeman."

"When was the last time you saw her?"

"I'm not sure of the date but it was at night around midnight, about two months ago."

"What was she doing at that time?"

"When I saw her, she was sitting in the living room, she told me to go back to bed and I did. When I woke up, she was gone."

"Does she have any nearby friends or family?"

"No, we live out in the country, there's really nothing nearby."

"Can you provide an address?"

The questioning proceeds, and Odessa provides as much information as she can. Finally, the officer says, "It's not a lot to go on, but we have enough information to begin the investigation. The description you provided will do but if you can bring in a photo that would be best."

"Okay officer," Arizona says. "Thank you for all your help. Other than bringing in the photo, is there anything we can do?"

"Unfortunately, no. At this time, we just ask that you wait patiently."

"Okay, sir."

They turn to walk out then the officer stops Arizona. "Excuse me miss, can I speak with you for a minute alone?"

Lance takes Odessa to the car, while Arizona stays to talk with the officer.

"Ma'am, I didn't want to say this in front of the kid but typically when a person is missing for longer than a week, the likelihood of finding them alive decreases. And we are talking months in this case. I'm not saying this to discourage any of you but I wanted to prepare you in the event that we don't find her or if we find her under unfavorable circumstances."

"Okay officer, thank you for letting me know."

Arizona heads to the car, unsure of how, when, or if she should break this news to Odessa.

"Everything okay?" Lance asks her.

"Yeah, he just stressed the importance of getting a photo to him and his team." Arizona turns her head so that she could see Odessa sitting in the back seat. "Do you have one sweetie?"

"Not on me but I know where to find some."

"Where are they?"

Sheepishly, Odessa admits, "At my father's house."

Arizona's eyes widen as Odessa continues. "I kept a stash in a secret spot in my room at my dad's house."

"No way," Arizona exclaims. "I don't think that it would be a good idea to go there. Clearly, this man has a temper and for our safety I don't think we should entertain the thought of paying him a visit."

Odessa tries to reason with her. "But what if we go when he's not home? I know where the pictures are. It will take two minutes. I can slip in and slip out, and he'll never know."

"Absolutely not, Odessa. It's just too dangerous; we'll have to find another way to get a picture of your mom."

"How?" Odessa asks.

"We'll think of something," Arizona says and drops the subject. The car ride is silent until Lance speaks up.

"Is anyone else hungry? I could go for a pizza, and maybe a movie. How does that sound?"

Arizona responds, "That sounds like a great idea, I think I saw a pizza place near your house."

Lance replies, "Yeah I did too, Pizza Pipeline. If I remember correctly, their pizza is pretty good and they have flavored stuffed crust."

"That actually sounds really great." Arizona looks in her rearview mirror at Odessa, who is busy pouting. "What do you think, Odessa?"

"I'm not really hungry. I kind of just want to lie down."

"Really?" Arizona says.

"Yeah, got a lot on my mom, I mean mind."

"I understand."

Arizona turns on some music and they drive without speaking.

They pull into Lance's driveway after picking up the pizza. Arizona holds open the door, and Lance carries the pizza into the kitchen. He pulls out a stack of paper plates, while Arizona sets up in the living room, searching for a good movie on Netflix and rounding up some blankets.

Odessa attempts to head to one of the back rooms, but Arizona stops her. "Before you go lie down, please eat something, at least one slice."

Odessa grabs two slices and sits down at the dinner table while Lance and Arizona sit in front of the television watching a movie. Once Odessa's plate is clean, she heads to the back without even a glance in their direction.

Halfway through the movie, Arizona gets up to check on Odessa. Lance continues watching, but after a minute, Arizona charges back into the room, exclaiming, "She's gone!"

"What are you talking about?"

"Odessa. I've searched every room, she's not here."

"Where do you think she could have gone?" Lance asks.

"There's only one place I can think of that she would go and not tell us."

"You don't think she would…"

"Yes, she's probably halfway to her dad's house by now," Arizona says, exasperated.

"How; with what transportation?" Lance asks.

They rush to the window at the front of the house. They both sigh in relief; Arizona's car is right where she parked it.

"Maybe a bus? What if she hitched a ride with some stranger?" Lance said, worried.

"Come on, we have to find her," Arizona insists.

Arizona and Lance race to the car.

They drive around the area for a little while but don't see her anywhere.

Arizona speeds down the street and goes faster once she gets on the expressway.

Lance, holding on for dear life asks Arizona, "How do you know where to go?"

"Earlier, Odessa gave the address to the police officer, and I wrote it down. Remember, when I stepped away? Well, I was doing some research on where her dad lives. I didn't want to take any chances of running into him anywhere. It's almost two hours away but it's a straight shot north." She sighs. "I hope she's alright."

Lance begins to pray to himself. First, for safe travels, and second, that Odessa is safe and that her dad doesn't find her. "Amen."

The paved expressway turns into gravel as they near the house. Arizona announces, "We're almost there."

A muffled voice yells from the trunk of the Durango, "Good, it's getting stuffy back here!" Odessa pops her head up, then the rest of her appears as she climbs over to sit in the backseat. "And a bit cramped."

"Are you kidding me Odessa?!" Arizona yells. "I'm turning the car around right now."

"But we're here. It's the house to the left."

"Kill the lights," Lance says.

Arizona presses a button and it becomes pitch black. The only light visible comes from the porchlight of the house. She drives off the road slightly and creeps closer until the car is camouflaged by the nearby woods. They are close enough to see but not be seen.

"I can't believe it still looks the same," Odessa whispers.

Seething, Arizona spits out, "I've been worrying, praying that you were not in any danger, hoping your father didn't place his hands on you. And all this time, you were in the back!"

"Arizona, calm down, there is no sense getting upset at her," Lance says.

"What do you mean? I'm the one who drove us here; if anything happens it's on me. I'm mad at myself for being so impulsive." She does not want to admit it either, but she feels a bit stupid for getting outsmarted into doing the one thing she was against.

Lance says to Odessa, "Now that we're here, what's the plan?"

"My dad doesn't like to be home very much. Every evening around eight o'clock, he leaves to go to the bar for a few hours." They all look at the clock. 7:45. "The back window is busted and doesn't close all the way. It's just big enough for me to squeeze through. I can sneak in, grab what I need to and get out before he gets back."

"Okay," Lance says. "Whatever you're going to do, you need to do it fast."

"Lance, go with her," Arizona instructs, "just in case."

No one objects. Lance and Odessa sneak up to the house, watching out for any cars. When they see nothing for several minutes, they proceed to the back window. Lance boosts Odessa up, and she crawls through, landing in the bathroom. She peeks around the bathroom door, making sure the house is empty. A few lights are left on, so the house is not completely dark.

She speaks through the window, letting Lance know she'll be right back. Down the hall and to the left is her room. She heads inside to her secret spot, a loose floorboard under the leg of her bed. "No, no, no, no, no." The pictures are not there. "Are you serious?" She feels around in the empty space; nothing. Just as she was about to search somewhere else, she hears a door shut. Wide eyed and in a panic, she scoots under her bed.

Before she gets too far, she hears Lance's voice, whispering, "Odessa."

She runs into the hallway, and sees Lance standing there. "You nearly gave me a heart attack, what are you doing here?"

"You were taking a long time, I wanted to make sure everything was alright."

"How did you know the door was unlocked?"

"I tried it, and it opened. Is everything alright?"

"No, I looked in my secret spot and the pictures aren't there. I'm going to check in my dad's room, can you look out here?"

Without saying a word, he starts looking around, while she heads to the back. Lance has just about searched the entire front room when he hears a faint sound. His heart drops at the thud of work boots stomping up the stairs. He scans the room for the nearest hiding spot; with seconds left, he ducks behind the island in the kitchen.

Odessa's dad shuts the door behind him and heads straight for the counter to set a case of beer down. Grabbing a can, he plops down on the couch. Lance hears the can as it clicks open, which only makes his heart pound faster. All of a sudden, a ringing noise echoes throughout the house. He hears it again. It does not register that it's the doorbell until the man gets up and heads to the door.

"Who are you, what do you want?" he yells out.

Lance recognizes the next voice. *Is that...? No, Arizona.*

"Hello sir, I lost my dog and I was wondering if you've seen him around?"

"I haven't seen no dumb dog," Odessa's father answers gruffly, while he attempts to slam the door, but Arizona persists.

"Are you sure? It's an Alaskan Husky, with one brown eye, one blue, and salt and pepper hair."

Lance takes that as his opportunity to sneak to the back. He crawls around the island and at the precise moment when he is out in the open, in plain sight heading towards the hallway, a floorboard squeaks. Odessa's dad turns around to see Lance on his hands and knees. Arizona pushes in the door, knocking the man off balance. Lance runs towards Arizona, and Odessa's not far behind.

Her dad gets up just in time to grab the collar of Odessa's shirt. He yanks her down to the ground. "Odessa, is that you?" her dad asks.

Her eyes widen in terror. She takes a second to look past him at Lance and Arizona, and then her eyes shoot back to the burly man. He steps closer to her, with a grimacing look. "You look just like your mother."

Before he gets too close, Lance jumps on his back. The man runs backward into the wall and Lance drops to the floor. Arizona runs to Lance who is semi-conscious. Odessa's dad walks past Odessa to his room and disappears. Odessa crawls to her friends, just as her dad appears with the pictures of her mother in one hand and a gun in the other.

"I take it you are looking for these." Her dad waves the pictures in the air. She runs towards him, in an attempt to grab them but before she gets close enough, he points the gun at her. "Not so fast." He looks at the pictures. "I haven't seen you in months, kiddo, and all of a sudden here you are, with back up. And you don't even have the decency to say hello to your old man."

"I just came here for the pictures, hand them over, you drunk."

"Hey, hey, that really hurts my feelings. I've been worried sick sweetheart, wondering where you were and if you were okay. The last time I saw you," he said, waving the gun at Lance, "you were with that clown over there."

"I just want the pictures, and then we'll leave."

"Oh, come on now, don't be like that, we're all friends here."

"Give me the pictures!"

"Why would I do that, when they're the only thing I have left to remember your mom?"

Lance gets up to stand in front of Odessa, shielding her from the gun-wielding psycho. Odessa shouts from behind him, "I'm glad mom got away from a monster like you!"

"Got away, what are you talking about?"

"Mom left you. I'm sorry she ever met a heartless monster like you in the first place."

"Do you really think I would allow your mother to leave me?" her father sneered.

"Then where is she?"

"Out back in the shed where she's been since I killed her," her dad says with a callous grin. His grin widens as Odessa's face turns pale and her knees buckle. Arizona catches her before she hits the ground.

Lance charges at him while he's distracted by his daughter. They wrestle for the gun. It pops twice, then slides across the room in front of Arizona, who is clutching her stomach. Odessa grabs the gun and her dad runs out the back door.

Blood stains Arizona's top, and then the floor, as it pours from her wound. Lance rushes to her side and Odessa grabs the phone, dialing 911.

"My friend was shot, send help!" She gives them the address and demands that they hurry.

The paramedics wheel Arizona into the back of the ambulance and speed off to the nearest hospital. Lance and Odessa follow behind in the Durango. The police are waiting for them when they arrive. Arizona is taken back to the ER and Lance and Odessa are stopped in the lobby for questioning.

"Look, I know you've been through a lot within the last couple of hours. But we need to get a statement from both of you," an officer tells them. They spend the better part of the night retelling what happened and answering questions. Finally, just before dawn, the police finish with them and soon after, they are allowed to see Arizona.

Lance and Odessa stand next to Arizona's bed. She opens her eyes, smiles briefly when she sees them and then closes her eyes to rest for a few minutes. After five minutes, she reopens them only to find Lance and Odessa glued to the television. "Hey guys, what's up?"

"Arizona!" Odessa's eyes beam with joy as she rushes to her friend and embraces her with a gentle hug.

"What are you guys watching?" Arizona asks.

Lance speaks up, "The news. Look at what's happening."

The three of them watch as the newscaster describes how Odessa's father was found passed out in someone else's car and was later identified as a man involved in a murder case. The news lady reports that the remains of Odessa's mother had been found in the shed behind the house, just as he'd confessed the night before. Lance quickly changes the station.

"That's enough of that," he says.

"I'm so sorry," says Arizona, placing her hand on Odessa's.

"I know," Odessa replies quietly.

Lance places his hand on top of theirs. "I know this might not mean much, but you have us, and if you think about it, we're like your family."

She stretches her arms around him and gives him the biggest hug. Tears trickle down her cheeks. Arizona tries to comfort her from her position on the bed and the tears begin to flow freely.

Odessa thinks about the family that never was and never will be. But a greater thought soon takes hold. She has a family right here and has had them this whole time. These people have been through hell and the hospital for her. Odessa is overwhelmed with thankfulness for them and slightly sad that she had not realized this until just now.

EPILOGUE

Arizona is not in the hospital for long. Three days after arriving, she is released to go home. Lance pulls up close to the hospital doors and helps load Arizona into the back seat. Lance and Odessa, from the passenger seat, discuss how the doctors were unable to remove the bullet due to its location.

"It's a good thing it missed all major organs," said Odessa.

"I guess this makes you Bullet Girl, Iron Man's distant relative," Lance jokes.

Arizona, however, does not laugh at his lame jokes. Instead, she rolls her eyes and sighs, facing the window. Lamenting over the bullet inside of her, she wonders how this will affect her life going forward. *If I travel, I bet the metal detectors will go off. Just like they would at ball games.*

"Arizona," Lance shouts loud enough to grab her attention.

"Huh?"

"Stop worrying, the doctors said you were well enough to continue your daily activities. You can even hike the Appalachian mountains if you want."

"Yes, I know. I'm not thinking about my health."

"Then what's on your mind?" he asks.

"I just never thought I'd ever have a bullet lodged inside of me, just chilling. I never thought I would get shot and live to tell about it. I'm grateful above all things but I'm scared too. What if the doctors miscalculated and it ends up moving an inch over, then what?"

"Then we pray that doesn't happen and only worry about it if it *does* happen. Enjoy today, for the things of tomorrow will be waiting for us tomorrow," he advises with finality.

"You're right Lance. That's very true," she says in a defeated tone.

"You know what, I'm not going to take you home just yet. We're going on a little adventure."

Odessa yells, "Road trip!"

"Going home would have been the road trip," Arizona corrects. "Do you know where we are, Lance?"

"Yeah, at the crossroad of adversity and adventure. Just sit back and enjoy the ride."

"Oh Lord, Jesus! Help us."

In unison, both Lance and Odessa say, "Amen."

Instead of taking Arizona home, Lance decides to go to a nearby park that has fresh flowers in abundance, and where birds could be seen flying all around, in the water, and in every tree in sight. When they arrive, Arizona steps out of the car and closes her eyes, smiling, to feel the sun caress her skin. The warmth feels good, the sounds of nature all around reviving her.

"This is amazing," Arizona says.

"Hold on, there's more," Lance says while pulling out a picnic basket and a blanket.

Arizona's grin reaches from ear to ear. "Oh, my goodness, are you serious?"

"I remember your story about you and your grandmother, and how you would have picnics and read the Bible. So, Odessa and I made a quick trip to a nearby shop and picked up a few things."

Odessa chimes in, "We knew this was a bummer for you, so we thought this might cheer you up. Were we right?"

Still beaming with joy, Arizona looks at them both and embraces them in a group hug. "You two are the best!"

"We know," Lance says with a satisfied grin.

Breaking away, Odessa says, "Hey, you two, enough chit chat; the goodies are getting warm." She snatches the basket out of Lance's hand and heads to a spot in the open field.

Odessa shouts behind her once she's at the chosen location, "Come on, I think I found a good spot."

Lance rolls out the blanket and the three of them sit down. Odessa sets up the food, handing each person their own sandwich, chips and a chocolate-chip cookie. In addition to the food, Odessa pulls out a Bible and they each take turns reading their favorite verses and stories, eating, and enjoying the time together amongst the flowers, birds, and sunshine.

During the merriment, Arizona thinks back to all those months ago, before she'd met Lance, when she used to be an emotional mess. Today she is proud to be able to say, "Kurt who?" She never used to let anyone get close to her, but now she understands the importance of her personal tests and trials; which afterwards came joy, and peace, and newness of life. Though what she went through at times drained her emotionally and physically, it would have sucked even more to have remained where she was and not allow God to work in His divine way, making her better. For the three of them, today marks a new beginning, where fear no longer has a hold on them. They have faith, love, and family, and because of that, they have all they need.